IDEEHO TALL TALES, ETC.

Darrell Davis

Ideeho Tall Tales, Etc.

Darrell Davis

Published 2025

Copyright © by Darrell Davis

Front Cover Art by Lacey Schmidt
Cover photo by Rachel Myers
Author's Photograph by Kathy Davis

Human Created Symbol of Distinction

ISBN 979-8-218-68682-6

Table of Contents

Hard Day Begins with Successful 765 Yd. Shot with 45/70

A slightly, well maybe greatly embellished tale of my 2020 deer hunt - Any resemblance to truth contained in this tale is purely accidental, but it is protected by a copyright by the author.

Last time I'll do that! There I was 3:13 am, eyes barely able to open after 6 middle of the night trips to the little boy's room, boy those seats are cold, to rid my system of the leftovers "served" up at the low budget outfitters hunting camp I'd been coerced into signing up with for what was promised to be a once in a lifetime Ideeeeeeho white tail hunt.

How was I to know that, "once in a lifetime" almost became reality after eating what the outfitter/wrangler/cook/?guide???, served up for my first horse camp "meal."

I have my suspicions that those leftovers were in fact leftovers from the previous hunt which ended two weeks earlier with the local mountain search and rescue team bringing in some additional horses and heavy equipment to search for and transport the hunters/victims to the local hospital from which the victims were life flighted to the nearest critical care center some 4 hours distant, by air.

Anyway, as I said, "last time I'll do that" and were it not for the fact I achieved some measure of success, I'd be more than a little ticked. After all, $20 per day, plus the extra costs/rent that went into making the "experience," "(food – using the term loosely, - sleeping bag, cot, tent, guide- again I use the term loosely, - hourly rent for the meat pole, etc. etc. etc.)," ain't just pocket change for a working man like myself.

I won't even go into needing to use my personal credit card to get enough fuel in the "guides" peekup to get out of the little Podunk town where the regional airport was located. I'll not go into detail, but have you ever been strapped into a tin can and thrown over one of those Western mountain ranges? That in and of itself was an experience, and by my count the 5th of the understatements contained in this report up to this point.

So, there I was, 3:13 am and the "cook/guide" was banging the bottom of an old metal pot with a large metal spoon when a nice cup of steaming coffee placed alongside my rented cot and sleeping bag might have served as a wake-up call just as nicely.

"Come and get it, come and get it, before I throw it out." Had I only known then what I was to discover over the following hours, the second option was the one I should have chosen! I can only say that thankfully T.P., rough as it was, was included in the $20.00 per day cost of the hunt.

But on to the pre hunt breakfast. There I sit, plate heaped full of what might have started out to be eggs, swimming in a pool of what I found out later to be grease from the grease pot which was on its 4th year of hanging from a convenient tree during the off season.

I might have skipped breakfast all together were it not for the fact that we, the other "hunters" and myself, were informed that lunch was a do-it-yourself "meal" the ingredients of which were contained in little brightly colored foil packets heaped up in the center of the breakfast table. That is, they were heaped up when we first entered the cook tent but now with the temperature slowly coming up to something above freezing, the packets seemed to be slowly dispersing over the top of the table.

A couple had even worked themselves over to the edge of the table, after which they fell to the dirt floor below. Don't hold me to it, but I could almost swear that I heard a chorus of painful cries coming from those two foil packets after they impacted the dirt floor. Strange, but the slow yet steady movement of those packets when they were still on the table top stopped immediately after those anguished cries ceased.

In retrospect, I might have been well advised to not eat the "eggs." As the old saying goes, you get what you pay for.

On to the hunt, When the "guide" slapped me on the back, forcing me face first to the ground with my nose plunged into the fresh and still steaming raisin like morsels, I knew we were on to something, a fact that was confirmed as soon as I got the larger raisin like morsels cleared off my glasses.

There it stood, the trophy of a lifetime. The goal of my once in a lifetime Ideeeeeeho hunt. A huge trophy White Tail buck. Still trying to get the remainder of the green slime from the raisin like morsels cleared off my hands and glasses, my efforts were slightly delayed in accessing my rangefinder. During those few moments the trophy buck increased the range between us, the cook/guide and myself and himself, the buck, by an estimated 437 yds., before he finally stopped, offering a classic broadside shot which then measured exactly 765 yds. distant.

Seemed a bit close, but the guide/cook said I'd better take the shot as trophies like this one don't happen along every day. So, attempting to elevate myself far enough above the green raisin like morsels to allow for my day pack to be used as a rifle rest, I hunkered down to take the shot at my trophy of a life time.

Once more verifying the distance with the rangefinder and hoping the light green smears on the lens, were not fouling up my measurement, I prepared to take the shot. The concern being that should that green smear increase or decrease the measured distance by just a 100 yds. or so, it might put me off target by just enough to miss this once in a lifetime opportunity.

Well, the shot was made. The slight amount of Kentucky windage employed being right on and as they say, now the fun was over and the work begins.

Really considering everything, things at this point were not so bad as they might have been. The guide/cook had taken a fall, saying later something about the muzzle blast from the 45/70 knocking him off his feet which then caused him to fall back over a conveniently placed windfall measuring about 3' at the butt. The fall causing him to break both legs, which left him less then helpful during the field dressing process.

Admittedly, it was a bit of a struggle getting the guide/cook and my once in a life time trophy buck out in one trip, and in truth I did give some thought to just putting the feller out of his misery as it would have made him much easier to drag.

However, I can't see that he had much to complain about as attaching ropes to both feet and dragging him the 9 miles back to camp assured that the bones in both legs were nicely aligned when he got to the hospital.

There might have been some issue with the left arm which kept hanging up in the brush. That factor being especially bad the one time his arm hung up in the crotch of a windfall and I had to pull especially hard to get him clear.

The fact that I had to pull really hard at times, especially when going uphill, was a blessing from my point of view as he seemed to decrease the number/loudness of complaints at such times. At other times I had to sing really loudly to keep the complaints from distracting my efforts to get us both safely back at camp.

Yep, guess all in all and in spite of the conditions mistakenly signed up for on the low budget Ideeeeeeho hunt, it turned out to be at least in some measures a successful hunt.

Best to ya all,

The Crusty Deary Ol'Coot

P.S. Just received a note from the outfitter's wife saying that her husband should be out of the hospital and into rehab in another 6 weeks. Looks like he'll walk again, but the left arm has been a bit of a challenge. I likely should have attached a third rope to that arm considering that the traction on the legs worked out so well. Oh well, live and learn.

CDOC

The Misguided Misadventures of Chinook and Laroy

Chapter 1

Once upon a time, in the far off hills of North Idaho, back in the days when men were men and women were,------ Well men were men, lived a couple of young lads, name of Chinook and Laroy.

Now the boys were none to bright, even as North Idaho boys of the time went, neither being what might be called the brightest match in the box. However, both boys seemed to grow and progress at what could be called a reasonable rate, considering the area and the somewhat questionable period of history.

Speaking in relative terms here, Laroy did seem to have a bit sharper point on his pencil, far out pacing Chinook academically, which enabled him to successfully complete his second year in the 3rd grade by the time he was only 15.

Seemingly this situation didn't dull the friendship of the two boys, possibly because Chinook being considerably larger and stronger than Laroy was able to carry the lion's share of camping gear needed for the numerous back country excursions on which the pair regularly embarked.

Chinook was the largest boy in the 1st grade by far, towering over his class mates by at least 3' and out weighing the closest competitor by all of a hundred and ten pounds.

Chinook, again possibly because of his size and proximity to the front of the classroom, did seem to catch the eye of the new teacher of the one room school house that year, and it did appear for a time that something like a romantic relationship might be forming.

This romantic possibility however, did seem to move into the category of remote after one of the new teachers three school dresses was permanently fouled by her fall into the outhouse hole late one cloudy and dark Friday afternoon.

Having made the same trip earlier in the same day, and done so with no more disastrous results then what might be considered normal for the time and considering that Chinook was the only person remotely big and strong enough to have moved the outhouse the three feet needed to expose the pit, the teacher's ardor seemed to cool from that point on.

Too bad, as it seemed for the first time that Chinook was a sure thing to make second or maybe third grade at the end of that school year.

This turn of events didn't really seem to negatively impact Chinook, possibly because he had as yet to begin understanding the full scope of the male/female relationships. In fact, it had been quite troubling to him that the new teacher didn't have her hair done in pig tails.

In truth, if there was one thing that really troubled him about being in the 1st grade, it was the fact that being seated in the first row in that one room school house meant that all the girls with pig tails were seated either beside or behind him. Stay tuned for the further adventures of Chinook and Leroy.

The Misguided Misadventures of Chinook and Laroy

Chapter 2

When we last checked in on the less then dynamic duo, we found Chinook facing public disgrace and censure by the local school board after the teacher's rather graceless plunge in to the school's outhouse pit. This proved to be a situation which left no lasting or even short-term impact on the teenager, his seemingly limited mental capacity still being much occupied with the strange and as yet unexplained feeling for girls in general, and specifically those with pig tails.

Yep, to Chinook's way of thinking if the recently departed and one term teacher of their single room school house would have sported pig tails, she indeed would have been a fine one. Maybe even a keeper.

Sad though it be, that Chinook must once again return to the 1st grade, the school board had unanimously decreed during their final and closed-door meeting of the year, that this simply could not continue unabated.

Chinook's physical advancement, while far out distancing his mental, had reached a point where not only were there no desks below 8th grade level, large enough to accommodate him, his sheer size seated in the first row was blocking the teacher's view of a dozen or more students in the second, third, fourth and fifth grade rows.

Seated behind him, the only student easily and readily seen in those rows being his pal, Laroy.

While Laroy was academically challenged to only a slightly lessor degree than Chinook, he did seem to be in possession of some, although limited, abilities involving manual dexterity, only grasping the finer points of skills like mule riding and campfire cooking of fine fare such as fried Slammie after much time and repetition of instruction invested by none other than Chinook himself.

Not only that, but it was widely known that Chinook had been instrumental in finally persuading Laroy of the benefits found when the rider of large four-legged critters chose to face the direction of travel taken by that critter. Something which to that point, Laroy had failed to grasp or possibly had chosen to ignore.

The turning point likely came the day when during an extended ride, Laroy was swept off his mule by low hanging branches for the 5th time in less than two hours, the final time resulting in a broken leg and numerous other bruises and sprains.

The reason why Laroy had persisted in riding, while facing South on a North bound mule, was never entirely clear, but it was thought that possibly the fixation on the less then glamorous and polite parts of the mule family might have something to do with his seeming attachment with skunks. Just maybe there was some sensual reminder there, to the half dozen or more, black and white stripped pelts he had nailed to his bed room wall.

However, never let it be said that Laroy wasn't able to finally grasp and retain the finer points of things academic or physical, after all, he was proudly advancing to the 4th grade at the beginning of the next academic year.

Sadly however, Chinook just didn't seem to get it academically. "It" being loosely defined as anything containing letters of the alphabet or numerals where anything greater than, 3, or any combination of multiple numbers were employed.

Finally, after a couple hours of head scratching and indecision, it was decided by the school board, that if only for the reason of Chinook's rather high level of manual dexterity, he would without question be advanced to the 2nd grade, but only after the following years school term. Providing that is, if he would but fulfill three requirements during the upcoming school session.

> #1. Chinook must faithfully beat and clean the chalk board erasers twice a day for the entire school year.

#2. Chinook would refrain from again moving the outhouse in any manner which would require the school district's buying and replacement of a teacher's shoes and dress, not to mention the varied and assorted other garments.

#3. Chinook would from hence forth, refrain from pulling any pig tails, which might be attached to or in evidence on any girls or women.

Could things possibly get any worse for the two? Stay tuned and see.

The Misguided Misadventures of Chinook and Laroy

Chapter 3

School was out, the school board had, again, sent out a bulk mailing or maybe better said, a bulk pleading, for applicants to assume the position of next year's teacher for the Three Pines school.

It wasn't that Three Pines school was so terribly remote, the school house being located barely a quarter mile outside the city of Three Pines, but it was safe to say that due to certain factors, the school had begun to develop a rather wide-ranging reputation for being, shall we say, academically remote.

The city of Three Pines was generally a rather happy and possibly somewhat sleepy town of about 437 persons, 27 Jack Russel terriers and an uncounted number of cats. That count being taken before the birth of the Gilbert triplets and the arrival of Bubba McCumber's family which numbered as nearly as anyone could figure, some 15 – 20 counting kids, brothers, sisters, one aged aunt and at least one mother-in-law The number of cats seems to be in a continued state of flux making counts difficult.

So, with the school being dismissed for the summer, there were those who hoped for summer employment opportunities to capture the attention of some of the less motivated student population, which from the county sheriff's point of view just might go a long way toward lessening the call outs to which he and his officers had been called upon to respond during the last four Summers.

While the sheriff's office had yet to have a "laying on of hands" in regards to the perpetrators, it was commonly accepted that the "perps" were thought to be one "Chinook" Greg Appleton and his co-partner/conspirator in all things out of control, "Laroy" Ron Jeffers.

The situation had advanced, or maybe better said, degenerated to the point where sheriff Clancy McMasters had called a general meeting of any and all citizens, organizations and persons of interest within North Range County.

He had almost resorted to hog tying the chairman of the Three Pines City Council, just to assure his attendance at the county wide meeting. Charlie Finnie's reluctance possibly being linked to his seat on the Three Pines school board, a group which had, in total, refused to attend the meeting in anything like an official capacity.

The total of commercial ventures within the city limits of Three Pines itself, numbered three and one half. The half being Calvin Smith's somewhat parodic operation of the local branch of, "Smith's War Surplus Things and Such. Smith's "operation" might or might not be open, possibly depending on the weather, mood of the owner/operator and upon his recent acquisition of any worthy yard/garage sale finds or the increasingly rare purchase and availability of actual, War Surplus items.

The other business, while dependably "open", were more of the mom & pop verity and consisted of Shorty's Gas and Garage, Inc., Missy's grill and Suds and the all-important general store, Mort and Sally's One of Everything Emporium.

So, it was not with a lot of optimism, that sheriff McMasters called the meeting to order, promptly at 7:00pm on the first Tuesday after the Spring dismissal of the Three Pines school.

Most of the local farmers had already hired and fired, some on more than one occasion, the persons of interest, while the three possible and viable retail or service operations in town were not likely to survive an increase of overhead and liability insurance such hiring's might entail.

Smith's War Surplus Things and Such, was not only intermittent in operation, and therefore not likely to hire summer employees, but it was suspected that in fact Smith himself might be an enabler to certain less then positive actions on the part of person or persons suspected but as yet "officially" un- named.

The only possibly positive outcome of the meeting was a suggestion by Granny Sue Ann, that it might be wise to set up a, "fund."

That fund being made possible by contributions from interested parties of which there seemed to be many, and included contributions from the sheriff's department and the city of Three Pines. The fund being divided equally between Mort & Sally's and Smith's War Surplus Things and Such and drawable in the form of goods by parties as yet un-named.

The goal, to facilitate the prolonged summer absents of certain parties within the county.

While McMasters had some reservations as to the viability of the suggestion, Charlie Finnie was heard to mutter something about the legalities of designating city funds for personal use, it seemed to be the only positive suggestion which came from the 4-hour meeting. Most of the other suggestions likely involving jail time for numbers larger than the total capacity of the county lock up.

Will it be "up a lazy river" for Chinook and Laroy? Stay tuned.

The Misguided Misadventures of Chinook and Laroy

Chapter 4

"Come on Chinook, Uncle Jimmy has his truck run'in and ain't wait'in much longer. We gotta go, now—NOW, ya hear me, hurry or we'll miss our ride to the trail head!"

Laroy was having real questions about his long-time friend and partner's strange behavior. Something which had shown progressive signs of deterioration ever since that teacher had started to lay those big brown moon eyes of hers on him sitting there in the first-grade row of the one room school house.

There he stood, just like Kalijah the wooden Indian, Mort and Sally's teenage daughter, Sally Mae having already charged out their camping supplies against their pre-paid credit account, was now waiting for Chinook to put his "X" on the line of their monthly charge summery card to show that it was indeed, one of them which had picked up all the grub.

Seemed like lately Chinook was almost more trouble than he was worth at times. What was he thinking? That mere slip of a girl didn't stand an inch over 5' and that set of pig tails reach'in half way to her waist was sure to get caught up in every tree or scrub within 10 yads of the trail.

Why it was as plain as the freckles on her face that she was just trying to provide first class customer service by asking all those questions about the 3 cases of Slammie and the bag of spuds they'd just brought to the checkout counter. There was no way she could pack her fair share of gear, let alone the extra 2 cases of Slammie required to feed her should she decide to tag along.

No sir, what Chinook needed was a big gulp of fresh air to clear his system of that funny flowery smell that seemed to follow Sally Mae's every step.

"We're burn'in daylight," Laroy hollered at Chinook as he ran for the door. "Uncle Jimmy is half way out of the park'in lot, let's go!"

Now, two hours from the trail head, Laroy was having second thoughts about his yelling at Chinook and the wisdom of his grabbing and shouldering that canvas 6 man tent they'd let Ol'man Smith talk em into charging against their credit at Smith's War Surplus Things and Such.

Maybe the tent, heavy as it was, would have been OK, but the way his skin was leak'in he was beginning to have additional second thoughts about the foldable/packable/portable combination heat and cook stove they also charged at Smith's. That just might have been a deal or possibly better said, a back breaker.

If it wasn't for the fanning of the trail side bushes and the rushing air currents, his repeated gasps for air seemed to be causing, which in turn and thankfully gave some slight relief from the megawatts of heat his tortured muscles were releasing in a cloud like mist all about him, he'd be of a mind to call it all off and head back to town to rake Mrs. AJ Broadmore's lawn. Maybe work wouldn't be so bad after all. Well, maybe not.

Scraping the leakage from his brow and out of his burning eyes, Laroy could just barely make out the form of Chinook bounding up the trail ahead. Looked like Chinook was about to the top of the first pass, only three, gasp gasp more to go. Maybe next time he'd leave those steel tent poles at home.

Seemed like nothing could slow Chinook down once he got his head cleared of the terrible smell they endured while picking up supplies at Mort & Sally's. Guy could always get those smells, should he ever in a weaker moment desire to do so, just by spending a Spring afternoon laying around over in Frank Jones' apple orchard. Plus, there was always the possibility of the odor being mitigated to some degree by the moderating influence of the Clossner's dairy operation.

Seemed that Chinook had the bit firmly in his teeth in spite of the 3 cases of slammie and 25lbs of spuds, various and assorted other food items, salt & pepper, matches, sleeping bags and fish poles etc. etc. he had lashed onto his pack frame.

But frankly what bothered Laroy at this point, even more then the fact that mud was starting to ball up around his ankles, the result of the copious leakage from every pore on his body, was that silly grin he'd seen Chinook wearing when they left the trail head.

It was beginning to worry Laroy a lot. Something was indeed wrong with his longtime pal!

Will the clear mountain air bring Chinook back to his senses? Stay tuned.

The Misguided Misadventures of Chinook and Laroy

Chapter 5

Waaaaaap SPLASH! Laroy turned around just in time to see Chinook begin to rise from the water like some great white and hugely oversized gnome, that silly grin firmly in place on what had been up until recently, a rather normal if not handsome face for a teen age boy.

Yep, this was beginning to worry Laroy a lot.

The hike into Pardon Us Mama had, considering, been rather uneventful. The "considering" including the fact that Chinook had outpaced Laroy by two hours and twenty-seven minutes on the walk in, had never once turned around or come back to ascertain the reason for his pals seeming predisposition for lagging behind and the fact that Laroy was forced to prostrate, himself a dozen or more times at stream crossings to replenish the copious amounts of fluids which had leaked from his every pore.

Now, not only did Laroy leave himself open to a ravaging case of, "Beaver Fever" by drinking freely and repeatedly from the unfiltered water, but due to the weight of his pack, and the fact that he could neither get it on or stand up unassisted with the pack in place, each stop meant Laroy had to crawl through the stream, over to some hopefully convenient rock or tree and then claw himself up the rock or tree and back into a standing position.

The bright side of this situation was the fact that by crawling through the streams a dozen or more times, the flowing water did dissolve and flush away the accumulation of mud balls which tended to accumulate around the bottoms of Laroy's pants, and thereby he arrived at Pardon Us Mama lake in a rather more presentable condition then might have been expected.

The last stream being a mere 200yds. from the boy's proposed camp site on the shore of Pardon Us Mama, Laroy had simply crawled the final distance, choosing to give some hope that his remaining fingernails, might at some future date again fulfill their intended purpose.

Once Laroy had crawled the remaining distance into camp, Chinook was immediately on his feet with what appeared to be indignation that his partner would be so brazen as to lag behind in the hopes that he would already have the work of camp set up completed. Never mind that camp couldn't be, "set up" until the tent, tent poles and stove arrived.

As Laroy had laid there, peering out from under the edge of his over loaded pack frame, he was struck again by his friend's countenance, that silly lopsided grin seemingly permanently affixed.

Now, there was Chinook, chest deep in water cold enough to severely chill any and all unprotected parts of the body. Just standing there, not moving, grinning from ear to ear, looking more with every passing second as if his skin was taking on the color of the sky on a clear Spring Day.

"Get out of the water, you'll wreck the fish'in!" Laroy hollered from where he'd collapsed once the tent was up and the stove assembled. Boy was he ever going to let Ol'Man Smith from Smith's War Surplus Things and Such have an ear full when they got back to Three Pines.

Just to think he'd packed those steel tent poles all the way into Pardon Us Mama just to find out that the tent was one of those new-fangled Special Forces things that came prepackaged with light and flexible fiber glass tent poles. Made ya think that Ol'man Smith might be a tad less than 100% reliable.

Grabbing one of the unused and unneeded steel tent poles, Laroy reached across the gap between the rock, which marked Chinook's launching point into the lake, and his as yet un-moving friend as he attempted to prod him into some type of action.

"Move it Chinook! Get out of the water! There are already half a dozen big ones turned belly up behind ya! Any longer and there won't be any fish left in the entire lake!"

Maybe that was a slight over statement of the true facts, but Pardon Us Mama being quite possibly the premier Cut Throat waters here abouts, you just couldn't be too careful.

The strangely named lake didn't seem to get a lot of traffic, possibly because of the distance and elevation which separated it from better known waters, but more than likely due to the ghost of one of the sheep herders said to be instrumental in the naming of the remote body of water.

Seems, according to the story generally circulated, one day two grizzled old sheep herders happened on to the shore of the lake shortly after the arrival of a girl scout troop and their exhausted leader. Upon finding the quite comely lady skinny dipping to refresh herself, the sheep herders were said to have proclaimed, "Pardon Us Mama," after which they immediately took seats on the warm shore line rocks and proceeded to observe.

The story went on to say, that the unidentified lady was said to take some exception to these actions where upon she departed the water without bothering to protect her modesty and proceeded to use anything and everything within reach to beat upon the one sheep herder who had been so crass as to pause for one last look.

Anyway, ghost or no ghost, Pardon Us Mama was one great fish'in hole!

Will Laroy be able to get his friend out of the water soon enough, or will Chinook forever sing soprano?

Check back and see.

The Misguided Misadventures of Chinook and Laroy

Chapter 6

Tromp, tromp, tromp, tromp the incessant racket continued, tromp, tromp, tromp, tromp. The noise only dimming slightly when Chinook's "tromping" took him a hundred yards back along the shore line of Pardon Us Mama, before he turned once more and "tromped" back towards camp.

Clearly, trying to get any sleep at all was going to be a questionable endeavor at best. Laroy, his nose already being all which was visibly protruding from the war surplus mummy bag bought at Smith's War Surplus Things and Such, began to burrow his way head first towards the bottom of the offenders' sleeping bag in a hopeful attempt that the combinations of his and Chinooks bags combined would deaden the sound of the constant tromping that had so far successfully kept him awake.

Not only were Smith's war surplus mummy bags, NOT overly warm, but even two deep they weren't much for keeping out the sleep robbing extraneous sounds. Tromp, tromp, tromp.

If it hadn't been for the fact that Laroy's prodding had finally tipped Chinook over in the clear deep water, and just before dark a strong breeze had sprung up blowing Chinook's semi solid remains towards shore where Laroy could finally grab a leg and drag his friend into the shallows, he'd likely still be standing there today, still grinning, not moving.

It had taken all of three weeks' worth of wood burning at a furious rate, and Laroy almost 3 full hours of rolling hot rocks into the shallows on both sides of those portions of Chinook which he, as yet, had been unable to drag up the bank, before Chinook had finally moved and muttered his first word. Food!

Maybe he should have let that camp coffee cool off a tad before pouring a cup full, give or take a few swallows, straight from the pot into Chinook's gaping mouth. But considering the continuing state of his pal's facial expressions since earlier that morning, it had been a bit difficult to decide if he just looked like a baby robin, beak open for another load of second hand worms, or he was wanting a drink of the coffee Laroy had set to boiling a couple hours back, or did that grin just naturally look slack jawed when you were laying on your back, half in and half out of the ice cold Pardon Us Mama waters at 11:30 at night.

Laroy, was certain of one thing, forgetting to pour cold water into the coffee pot not only didn't do much to settle the grounds, but that over site also didn't greatly diminish the temperature of the semi solid brew. One way or the other, one mouth full of those hot coffee grounds had Chinook up and out of the water, spitting and coughing, hacking and growling, sounding and acting for all the world just like a she bear with a mouth full of porcupine quills.

Seems the only peace and quiet Laroy had been able to enjoy since his partner had regained his footing had been those few moments between filling Chinook's tin plate with delicately prepared and golden-brown slices of sautéed Slammie, and when the loud and repeated demands for "more" recommenced, each word accented by a loud banging on the bottom of the tin plate with Chinook's only slightly smaller than mouth sized, eat'in utensil.

By the time the consumption of what had been a two-week supply of a camping staple had ceased, Chinook had grazed his way through 14 cans. At least and thankfully that stupid grin had been replace! Or had it? Possibly it had just been disguised by the rapid jaw movements, which considering that Slammie was packaged in a pre-chewed slurry made from the residual floor sweepings after the production of hot dogs and bologna, the mixture than brought to a semi stable and solid consistency by large amounts of heat applied during canning, well maybe the grin was just misplaced.

One way or the other, Laroy now had new worries. If the waters of Pardon Us Mama had been tainted to any negative degree by the hours of Chinook's semi-submersion, coupled with the rapid consumption of the one and only item Laroy was well versed in cooking, what had started out to be a two week stroll in the hills just might come to a rapid and abbreviated conclusion.

Little chance that Chinook's appetite was going to diminish any time soon, not with him just turning the corner and starting down the back stretch on mile number 6, every mile covered since he'd ceased feeding, stood to his feet, proclaimed, "full" and started the aggravating tromp, tromp, tromp, tromp shortly after 12:23am.

Good thing that brown eyed school teacher had taken it upon herself to pack her remaining 2 unsullied outfits, pocket the Three Pines school board's reimbursement for damages incurred on her 3rd outfit and caught the next weeks Gray Hound for parts unknown. Just maybe things would start to get back to normal before Summer was over.

Well then, maybe not. Laroy slowly began to fad off with images of blue eyed, freckled face Sally Mae smiling up at Chinook, smells like an apple orchid in full bloom with undertones of Clossner's prize Holsteins, wafting through the confines of that G.I. Mummy bag, tromp, tromp-------.

Had Chinook forever tainted the waters of Pardon Us Mama, or would fresh trout be on the menu for breakfast? Check back to see.

The Misguided Misadventures of Chinook and Laroy

Chapter 7

Laroy breathed in a deep breath of the frosty air as the second big Cut Throat of the morning slurped his size #14 Pardon Us Mama double ended purple and gold dry fly below the lakes surface.

Prospects had brightened considerably over the last few minutes, not only with the hopes of breakfast and the possibility of continuing the high-country pack trip, but with the increasing likelihood of having enough food to last out the entire two weeks after Chinook's recent mid-night binge.

The slight breeze which rippled the lakes surface had, for the most part, cleared away the smell of the hot shoe leather. Then with Chinook's collapse between two large boulders, half way down the back stretch, the "tromp, tromp, tromp, tromp" which had continually echoed, throughout the night, echoing back from the cliffs on the far side of Pardon Us Mama had also all but ceased.

The soft snoring sounds coming from Chinook's direction were actually rather soothing to Laroy's frayed nerves, closely resembling the quiet rippling sounds he heard as he was laying, ear deep and face down in the numerous creek crossings during yesterday's exhausting hike into the high country.

Now, if Chinook would just remain asleep long enough, and the fish would continue their ravenous attack on his dry fly for a few more minutes, maybe he could stringer just a few more fish. Meanwhile, the chances that breakfast would become a reality were improving by the second.

Laroy had never perfected the art of camp fire cook'in much beyond his production of golden-brown slices of beautifully sautéed slammie, but just how difficult could it be to fry up a mess of mountain trout? Especially consider'in the fact that there was all of ¾" of slammie drippings in the bottom of the skillet, the remnants of Chinook's gouge-a-thon of the previous night.

Pancakes, now that would really set the meal off in fine shape, but the last time Laroy had tried mak'in pancakes over a camp fire, Chinook made him promise to never attempt it again. Something about three visits to the oral surgeon having put Chinook's father off his feed for almost two weeks.

Come to think of it, that was the last time Chinook's dad had been able to find time to accompany them on one of their outings. Funny, it seemed that he'd really enjoyed camping before that trip.

SLURP!!!!!!!!!! The dry fly disappeared in the bottom of a crater nearly 2 feet across and all of half that in depth. Gone, along with Laroy's fancy one of a kind tapered leader which had been attached to his one and only copy of the #14 Pardon Us Mama double ended purple and gold dry fly.

Laroy sat down to survey the damage, opened his dry fly box and then began to examine the frayed end of his floating fly line. Must have been a big one!

Too bad Ol'Coot hadn't tied up a few more of that pattern, but the Ol'guy did seem a bit out of sorts the last time Laroy and Chinook dropped by to visit and replenish their supply of dry flies.

Seems that what was locally considered the one bright spot of the house hold, known locally by the initials of, "CB," Coot's wife, had once again and clearly, made it known that there would be no more dogs in her house, something which always tended to put the Coot into a bit of a funk.

From Laroy's view point, a bit of dog hair would have been much preferable to the mounds of feather and fur trimm'ins that seemed to accumulate knee deep in every corner of the reloading and fly tie'in room where Ol'Coot spent the bulk of his time.

Coot was clearly fighting a losing battle on at least two fronts, not only were his repeated pleas for a replacement for Simple Simon falling on deaf ears, but there was a move afoot to officially re-name his room, "The Sewing Room."

Seems bad enough that the guy would be forced to live out his declining years without a furry and four-legged critter by his side, but if word should get out that he was pursuing his hobbies and taking his daily nap in, "The Sewing Room," well seems as though most folk could easily understand how this could damage one's self-respect and standing in the community.

Will Chinook wake up, still grin'in? Will the Crusty Ol'Coot be allowed to maintain his self-respect in the local community? Will Laroy find a substitute for the #14 Pardon Us Mama double ended purple and gold dry fly and catch enough fish for breakfast? Stay tuned.

The Misguided Misadventures of Chinook and Laroy

Chapter 8

"Hurry up Laroy!" Chinook shouted over his shoulder for about the 14th time over the last mile.

"You forgett'in they close the doors at Mort & Sally's at 6 sharp? Get a move on!"

Laroy shook his head figger'in the good Ol'Days to be a thing of the past for sure. They still had two cans of Slammie left, the fish had remained willing to take a fly even if their one and only copy of the #14 Pardon Us Mama double ended purple and gold dry fly had departed early on.

However, in spite of there be'in plenty of food, typically the number one consideration for Chinook on any back-country adventure, he had been pacing and grin'in almost nonstop for the last three days.

He was almost normal, well maybe better said, "normal" for Chinook, once he woke up late the afternoon of their second day at Pardon Us Mama lake. But his condition had worsened steadily over the 4 days, beginning as best Laroy could determine the day some wild flowers came into bloom downwind from camp, and began to spread that sickening sweet odor over the whole area.

More Laroy thought about it, the more the odor reminded him of that strange smell back at Mort & Sally's. Come to think of it, Chinook hadn't been right starting the day Sally Mae had waited on them just before they headed into the hills. "Chinook keeps this up," Laroy muttered to himself, "think I'll get a mule." "Maybe a mule and see if CB will let Ol'Coot out of the house long enough to go camp'in." Something needed to happen and quick or the whole summer wound be a wash.

Summer would be over before they knew it at this rate, and they'd be back in Three Pines school house, he in his first year of 4th grade, and Chinook firmly entrenched in 2nd grade thanks to the actions of the school board, with Sally Mae sit'in 7 rows back in the 9th grade row.

Not only was summer coming down as almost a total loss, but the prospects for the school year seemed non too bright, what with Sally Mae spreading that discust'in scent over the entire school room as she and 30 yards of petty coats flounced their way from the door to her place at the back of the room.

Then there were the air currents caused by the incessant back and forth movements of all that lace as the teacher repeatedly called on Sally Mae to go to the chalk board and answer some silly question on math, why 4 times "X" equaled "Y" or why Texas was South of Minnesota or some equally ridiculous thing. As if anyone was likely to care anyway.

Rake'in Mrs. AJ Broadmore's lawn was look'in better and better.

Maybe a hunk of Limburger cheese hidd'in behind the woodstove come winter would help tone down that odor a bit. Funny how he'd never noticed that sweet smell before that day at Mort & Sally's when they were stock'in up for the hike into Pardon Us Mama.

Now there was Chinook, hot foot'in it back to Mort & Sally's like there was no tomorrow and them still with 2 fresh cans of Slammie in their packs and a lake full of fish just steps from the tent's door.

Well, at least he could be thankful that Chinook had offered to carry the camp stove and the steel tent poles back to town. But then it was really only fair, considering they had consumed all the spuds and most of the three cases of Slammie that had been hauled up the mountain.

Laroy turned the corner onto main street just in time to see Chinook shed his back pack and dash across the wooden porch and through the doors of Mort & Sally's One of Everything Emporium, leaving Mort standing by the door, key in hand.

"Land sakes boy," Mort gasp as he struggled to catch his breath, "you been sleep'in with a pole cat?"

"Take what ya want and leave quick. Ya can come back and sign the ticket after ya seen the flat side of a big bar of Grannie's Lye soap and a high-pressure hose but not before!"

Chinook was just lifting his pack to his shoulders after closing the flap over the top of his hastily gathered supplies when, "hi Chinook" kind of wafted softly over the air waves.

"You must be really strong to carry a big pack like that. You must be the strongest boy in the whole school. I'm having a party; would you like to come?"

There she stood the underlying reason for the aborted back country fish'in trip. Sally Mae, pink cheeks, blue eyes, eye lashes flutter'in like a humming bird's wings and thankfully up wind, all while Chinook's face was tak'in on the color of Three Pine's newest fire engine.

Yep, clear as the nose on your face, Chinook was a goner, but all in all and considering his present un-sanitized condition, maybe that flowery smell wasn't so bad after all.

Can Laroy find a new partner, will the twosome become a threesome, will Chinook regain his ability to speak? Stay tuned.

The Misguided Misadventures of Chinook and Laroy

Chapter 9

"Let me tell ya how it was back in the good ol'days," Ol'Coot said as he settled back in his rock'in chair, hooked his Vibram soled boots into the carpet and set the chair in motion.

"Yep, thems were the days! Criks full of fish bank to bank, deer behind every tree, girls pretty as the pictures in the monkey Ward catalog and every man or boy had a dog. Maybe two or three if'n he was lucky."

"NO, YOU'RE NOT GETTING A DOG!!!!!!!" The sound echoing and reverberating back and forth from wall to wall, room to room, slowly fading to a whisper over the next 3 to 4 minutes just as CB, towel in hand made an appearance at the door leading from the kitchen.

"If I've told ya once Coot, I've told ya a million times, we ain't havn'in no more dogs in this house and that's final. Over my dead body will another dog come to stay!

Laroy looked rapidly back and forth between Ol'Coot and CB. Should he ride it out or run?

He was sure as he could be that Coot's rock'in chair was now cycling back and forth at a much higher rate of speed then before. Boy, those Vibram soles could really dig in!

Seemed like Coot's weathered old face had settled into a slight grin and Laroy was sure he caught a wink as Coot smoothly slid the chair into the next higher gear.

"Easy there CB, ya know ya love dogs and are die'in to have a cute little critter keep'in your feet warm come even'in."

CB seemed to expand to new heights as she glared at her husband of far more years than she liked to count. "Coot, ya just listen up and I mean it. The only thing die'in round here will be you if you so much as think about bring'in a dog into this house, and I mean it!

The roll of carpet pushed up ahead of Ol'Coot's Vibram soled boots began to settle as CB turned to leave the room, causing Coot's rock'in chair to kick out of pass'in gear and back into cruise.

"wooooooo Wheeeee, weren't that someth'in? Now, where was I? Oh yes, yep good ol'days and every man had a dog ----------.

"COOT!, don't ya go there!"

No doubt about it now, Coot was grin'in ear to ear. Leaning in Laroy's direction Coot whispered, "tell ya a secret boy, pick yourself an older woman when it comes to marry'in time. It goes a long way toward keep'in life interesting. Yep that it sure do!"

"I hate ta interrupt ya just as the story gets to the interesting part," Laroy whispered back, "but I'm really worried about Chinook. He ain't really been his self ever since last school year, long about the just before the school teacher took that fall into the outhouse hole."

"Now he's got this stupid grin that won't go away and he just about walked my legs off com'in back from Pardon Us Mama lake. Couldn't wait to get back to Mort & Sally's and all he did when we got there was buy 6 more cans of Slammie and then stand there like a doofus when Sally Mae comes up and asks him to come to her party.

"Lucky she was stand'in up wind, as Sally's flower boxes had already started to wilt."

"Last I seen Chinook, he was still grin'in and stand'in chest deep in the Three Pines crik swim'in hole, bar of grammy Broadmore's lye soap in each hand and soap suds half way to the bridge.

"Hmmmmmmmmmm? Ya don't say?" Coot said while scratch'in his 3 days growth of gray stubble. Stand'in in the crik with 2 bars of lye soap ya say? Ya say this happened right after Sally Mae ask him to a party?"

"Yep, Mort ask Chinook if'n he'd been sleep'in with a pol cat, Sally's flowers started fall'in over like they were sort of water, Sally Mae showed up all fancy and smell'in like a Spring day in Frank Jones' apple orchard, and the next I knew Chinook has picked up two bars of lye soap from home and is stand'in chest deep in the swim'in hole in Three Pines crik."

"I ain't never seen Chinook pick up one bar of lye soap, let alone two bars and he only used to grin when eat'in my sautéed Slammie. I'm worried."

"Sounds a lot like he's act'in like a sick calf to me." Coot said as his Vibram's lost their grip and the rocker slowed to a stop. Can Chinook survive the aliment or will this be terminal. Stay tuned.

The Misguided Misadventures of Chinook and Laroy

Chapter 10

There he stood, Chinook, skin of face and neck nearly as pink as his shirt and tie which were set off by those white pants, pink socks and shiny white shoes. The pink socks kinda blending in to the pink of Chinook's legs where the pants and the socks didn't quite meet.

I'd never have believed it if I hadn't seen it with my own eyes when I cut down the alley behind Mort & Sally's on the way home from Coot and CB's place.

Yep, ain't never seen Chinook's skin take on that color and for sure never seen him dressed up like one of those circus dandies who come to town every year or so. So, there he was, flowers in hand stand'in on the porch of Mort & Sally's liv'in quarters back of the Mort & Sally's one of Everything Emporium.

I was just about to Mort & Sally's back gate when out steps Sally Mae, dressed up in one of those outfits that takes about 20 of those lacy petty coats to hold the bottom of the dress up almost waist high and a full three feet out in every direction.

How, if'n she wasn't a sight to behold, soft blue dress, light brown hair pulled back in one of those fancy dos, pony tails they call em, where the hair all turns up at the ends mak'in it difficult to get the ends into one of those ink wells they have on the desks over at the Three Pines school house.

Whoooo whee, fancy clear down to those little black shoes with the narrow straps over the matching light blue bobby socks. Believe it was the first time I'd seen a girl ware'in anything other than those high-top lace up school shoes.

Guess I'd have to admit, the effect complete to the soft smell of some kind of spicy and flowery fragrance wasn't half bad mixed in with the odor of Mrs. AJ Broadmore's lye soap.

Sure wish I could have seen what happened after that, but it was nearly a week before I saw Chinook again. This time, dressed in clean clothes, big apron clear down below his knees, broom in hand, sweap'in the front porch and steps over at the Emporium.

"Where ya been Chinook," I ask as I walked up to Mort & Sally's. "Ain't seen ya for near a week, what ya been do'in?"

"Been busy," Chinook muttered.

Color didn't look a bit good, still heavy overtones of pink visible even down to the skin show'in above his work boots. Eyes kind of glassy as he absently, mindlessly, looked off towards the mountains where we'd hiked into Pardon Us Mama lake.

"Bout time for another trip to the hills before school starts, don't ya think?"

"Busy." Chinook muttered again just as Sally Mae walked up beside him.

"Hi Laroy," she softly breathed, "how about you and Ronda Sue join'in Chinook and I for a picnic and swim over the swim'in hole after the store closes? Ma made some fresh peach pie and said we could take one with us. I can check with Ronda Sue if'n ya'd like."

"Tell ya what Coot," Laroy said as he settled into the rock'in chair on Coot & CB's front porch the next day. "There I stood, felt like I was backed into a corner and no place to run. Kinda just happened and before I knew it, I'd gone home slipped my swim'in trunks under my pants and was headed back to Mort & Sally's.

Went back to the Emporium and the first thing I knew; I was in the back room of Mort & Sally's. open'in cases, mark'in prices and stack'in the marked canned goods against the back wall. Hard to believe how much Slammie they go through, must have marked 20 cases. Chinook still not say'in much."

Bout that time Sally Mae and Ronda Sue come into the stock room to tell us it's quit'in time and they had the picnic lunch ready to go.

"Guess we walked, but didn't seem no time and there we was, splash'in water and swing'in out over the deep hole on the rope that's hung'in from the big ol'tree, girls gang'in up against Chinook and I and well was that peach pie ever good. With cook'in like that, maybe I can understand Chinook spend'in all that time over at Mort & Sally's"

"Tell me Coot, any idea how the girls get those swim'in outfits to look like that? Ain't never seen noth'in that compares cept the once I beat mom to the Sears and Sawbucks Spring catalog. Figured then it was just make believe, them try'in to sell lots of fancy clothes and all."

Coot's rock'in chair began to gather speed as the grin starts to spread across his whiskered face a far-off look coming into his eyes. "Yep Laroy, make believe, that's it, it's all just make believe."

Summers half gone, school's just weeks away, is Laroy going to come through unscathed? Stay tuned.

The Misguided Misadventures of Chinook and Laroy

Chapter 11

If it weren't for the fact of Coot's eyes be'in wide open and his legs continually propelling the ol'wooden rock'in chair at an ever-greater rate of speed, I'd thought sure as Chinook was act'in like a sick heifer, that Coot had fallen asleep.

The grin on his whiskered face could be the result of any number of conditions, asleep or awake, anything from having just gotten up close to one of CB's famous pot roasts to his having recently visited his hidden supply of 2-month-old apple squeezing's he hid out in the old wood shed.

"Might just as well go on home, Laroy," CB said as she stood observing her husband of more years than she liked to discuss. Coot's off on a trip some where's and it ain't likely he'll be back any time soon."

"He gets headed off on one of his trips and he might not get home afore morn'in. Jus no way a-tell'in."

"Make believe, that's it, it's all just make believe," Laroy muttered to himself as he walked through the warm Summer evening.

Catching himself break'in into a grin over the comment Ol'Coot made just before he left on, "his trip," he was sure of one thing. He liked what make believe had done for Ronda Sue and Sally Mae. Yes sir! Why when it came to make believe, this might even be better than Lincoln Logs.

Now if he could just get Chinook back to normal and get that silly apron off him along with that broom out of his hand, just maybe things could get back to normal. He'd about giv'in up on the grin, maybe it was an age thing. Kinda like with Coot.

Laroy couldn't recall hearing of even one outhouse be'in tipped over all Summer and nary a case, not even one, of clothes be'in switched from one back yard clothes line to another. Hadn't been one of the mayor's longies fly'in from the flag pole down at city hall come Sunday Morn'in for near 2 months, all in all, so far, a real boring Summer vacation.

With only 20 days before the bell would be ring'in up at the Three Pines school house, yep make believe or not, this was shaping up as a wasted Summer.

"Laroooooooy! Laroooooooooy, time to be roll'in out," his mother called. "Chinook's been pac'in the front walk for near 30 minutes. He's got half the dogs on the street worked up and bark'in, come on and get out of bed it's near 5:30 already.

There he was, Chinook, face all pink, apron almost long enough to hide the gap between his boot tops and the bottom of last year's school jeans. Back and forth, 8 or ten steps, turn 8 or ten steps back, turn, back and forth a look of dazed determination on his recently washed face, a bit of razor burn where days ago there was only a ragged display of accumulating stubble that give'in another 5 years might have become a respectable upper lip adornment.

"What ya want'in," Laroy growled as he staggered to the top of the front steps. "Ain't ya noth'in better to do than come round mak'in a commotion and wak'in everybody up in the middle of the night?"

"Want ta make 5 bucks?" Chinook said just before starting his return trip to the front gate.

"5 bucks, what do'in?" Laroy said, beginning to come to attention.

"Help'in the new teacher move in." Chinook replied as he paused slightly before again doing an about face. "School boards pay'in!" drifting back over his shoulders.

"School boards go'in to pay us, ya mean like hire us and this isn't work'in off no damages?" Laroy said in a questioning tone.

"Yep, their pay'in, Sally Mae's paw recommended me and I need some help. Miss Morgan's got a whole truck load arriv'in at 5:30," Chinook said as he paused one hand on the yard gate. "I got ta get move'in. Sally Mae and Ronda Sue are wash'in winders today and I need help unloading the heavy stuff. Ya go'in ta help or not?"

5:35am and there they stood, over at Jeb Frazier's rental watching the mov'in van back slowly towards the front porch.

Chinook minus the apron, face slightly less pink but eyes still retaining a good measure of somewhere far away.

"You boys here to work?" the truck driver asks. "if so, grab a box and get ta mov'in. I got ta get unloaded and back down the road before dark. The nearest motel is 50 miles back. Get mov'in what ya wait'in for?"

Chinook picked up a pile of boxes and headed up the ramp towards the front door, dazed or not, it didn't seem to have affected his strength in any negative way. Maybe all that sweep'in and stacking cases was even increasing his upper body fitness. Following in his friend's footsteps Laroy headed for the back of the house with a huge box marked bedroom.

Bending over to place the box next to a couple of suit cases, Laroy stood only to be confronted by the biggest pair of brown eyes he'd ever seen. Big brown eyes, long dark eye lashes, soft red lips, light brown hair to the shoulders and make believe beyond the pages of mom's latest catalogs.

"You must be Laroy," a soft voice floated to his ears apparently from the impossible vision before him. "I'm Miss Morgan, the new teacher. Mort said you and Chinook would be coming to help unload the truck this morning."

"Laroy, ------ Laroy honey, are you OK? Do you need to sit down, maybe some water?"

Jolted by a firm grip on his arm, Laroy followed Chinook back to the truck both eyes again beginning to track.

"Get a move on boys, I ain't got all day," the trucker growled.

"You OK boy?" he asks when he saw Laroy. "Your look'in like a sick calf? One eyes kind of off center like."

I need to talk to Coot, Laroy thought to himself as he picked up another box. Looks like "Make believe" is going to make for a long year.

First Chinook, and now Laroy. Can they possibly survive this malady? Stay tuned!

The Misguided Misadventures of Chinook and Laroy

Chapter 12

"Coot home from his trip yet?" Laroy ask CB a few days later when after hours of attempting to unravel the happenings of the Summer, he decided he needed the wisdom of someone with extensive exposure and experience with such things as, Make Believe.

Laroy had always thought it related to toys and sand box tractors, cap guns, beat'in the bad guys and comic books show'in some make believe action hero and later, there was attaching card board or play'in cards to wheel spokes on his bike and mak'in believe he was riding a motor cycle.

Now after a trip to the swimming hole along with Chinook, Sally Mae and Ronda Sue followed by help'in to move the new teacher, Miss Morgan, into Jeb Frazer's rental house he wasn't so sure. According to Coot, there just seemed to be a lot more involved with make believe then building roads in the sand pile behind Chinook's fathers' shop.

"Ya, weren't a long trip this time, Coot was back about an hour after ya went home. Funny thing though, don't know what you fellers was talk'in about, but Coot came back and had this strange far away look in his eyes almost like afore we got married."

"Paw had warned me about it before the wedding, but I never gave it much thought as it just kind of faded away over time, leav'in Coot about what I always considered to be his normal."

"You feel'in OK Laroy? Your eyes look a little glassy. Ya ain't been spend'in too much time in the swim'in hole have ya? Coot, --- come on out here, Laroy's got a question fer ya."

"Have a chair Laroy. Coot's been mov'in a bit slow last couple of days, but he'll get here if he ain't on another trip."

"Well, it's kind of likes I gots the flu only I don't." Laroy was attempting to explain to Coot some 20 minutes later, Coot having finally wandered onto the porch heading in the general direction of his rock'in chair.

Coot had a two handed death grip on his big old black coffee mug, the one which CB had attempted numerous times to wash, only to have Coot "rescue" it from her hands just before it fully submerged in the soap suds billowing over the top of the kitchen sink, Coot all the while complaining that it had taken him 35 years to get the cup broke in and he wasn't about to start over at this late date.

Coot's overly large cup, holding a full 16oz. of liquid in new or clean condition, which it wasn't, had sometime in the distance past begun to aid in decreasing Coot's intake of the road tar like brew he loosely referred to as coffee, the layer upon layer of stain having come to the point that Coot, at CB's last count, was now getting 23 "Cups full" from a 12 cup coffee maker.

Coot had one day accidentally bumped his cup up against the old wood trash burner sitting unused next to CB's new and shiny electric range, the impact chipping off some of the accumulated layers of stain and leaving the white of the original color blindingly shinning forth like head lights coming out of a tunnel at midnight.

Anyway, Laroy was attempting to explain to the Coot, the accumulated flu like symptoms that as best as he could recall, had stated about the time Sally Mae had invited him to join Chinook, Ronda Sue and herself for a picnic and visit to the swim'in hole.

He had only just begun to get over that experience when Chinook had used the $5 bribe to get him over to Jeb Frazier's rental to help Miss Morgan, the new school teacher moved in. "I ain't felt normal since." Laroy explained.

Coot had just powered his rock'in chair into cruse mode, Chewed and swallowed a couple hits from his coffee mug, his eye lids fluttering rapidly 6 or 8 times which seemingly cleared the glaze off his eye balls.

"Well Laroy," Coot began, "Make believe can affect a feller any nuber of ways, so I recon you ain't caught anything life threatening, even if it feels like it's terminal."

"Why I remember back about the time I first met CB, I'd just gots my driver's license and bought my first car, an old Ford 5 window coup, and my buddy Sammy and I decided to cruse over to the beach and hang out with a bunch of our school chums. Never did know why, but there wasn't a guy anywhere to be seen, just what seemed like every girl from our little high school class. Must have been 10 or so."

"There sat the ol'carry all that Janey Rea's parents let her drive. Janey Rea and some her friends had painted the old rig hot pink with violet fenders along with paint'in "Milly" across the back in big gold letters."

"Laroy, I ain't never seen that much "make believe" all in one place before or since and right in the middle of it all, there's CB coming out of the swim'in hole in a bright yeller swim'in suit. That suit was so bright it seared the image on my eye balls an I ain't never recovered."

As Laroy watched, Coot's eyes began to glaze over. Coot kicked the old rocker into high just as CB's voice could be heard com'in through the screen door. "Coot, don't you be tell'in tales out of school now ya hear. Laroy don't ya be pay'in any attention to his tales, the coffee done affected his memory of the true facts."

Fact or fiction, it was hard to tell from the ear-to-ear grin on Coot's face, but Laroy could almost see the image of "Make Believe" burned on his eyes, or was that his more recent image of Ronda Sue or Miss Morgan or --------------------?

First it is Chinook and now Laroy. Is it the water? Just what is to become of the once dynamic due? Stay tuned to find out.

The Misguided Misadventures of Chinook and Laroy

Chapter 13

There he was, first day of the new school year, slogging his way up the hill to Three Pines one room school house, feel'in like someone had just kicked his favorite coon hound, all while Chinook is walk'in up ahead loaded down with books, note books and other varied and miscellaneous school supplies. Washed to the point of glowing, almost to the level of Sally Mae, following her dainty steps like a 4H lamb going to the sale at Three Pines fair.

It wasn't that Chinook starting the 2 nd grade by degree of the Three Pine's school board, required that level of school supplies mind you, it was clearly a case of him somehow being enlisted to carry Sally Mae's school supplies along with an order from Mort & Sally's One of Everything Emporium to be delivered to the new school teacher, Miss Morgan.

Laroy kicked a rock, instantly regretting the action while walking head down contemplating the lost Summer just past. No out houses moved or tipped over, no fish'in trips to Pardon Us Mama lake, no clothes switched from clothes line to clothes line, none of the mayor's long johns flying from the city hall flag pole, all in all an almost total loss.

Why, the Coot hadn't even conned CB into allowing him to get a new dog even though three or four likely candidates had wondered through Three Pines during the Summer, some even being enticed to linger until CB found out that Coot was slipping them some dinner left overs.

Yep. Pretty much of a total waste of what could have been a really good Summer. CB kind of be'in set in her ways, well maybe there was an excuse for Coot's not having a new dog, but Chinook spend'in most all of the Summer at Mort & Sally's One of Everything Emporium, well it had been going on for so long that Chinook was begin'in to take on an underlying fragrance of something akin to what was even now wafting off Sally Mae's many layers of petty coats as she led Chinook towards the captivity of another school year.

Try as he might, the only bright spot Laroy could think of was that one trip to the swim'in hole with Chinook, Sally Mae and Ronda Sue when he'd been introduced to "make believe." Something that in spite of Coot's explanations he was still laboring to understand. Maybe if he could have kept Coot on track with his explanations as to the true depth of "make believe" he'd now have a better understanding of the situation. Seemed Coot was always leav'in on a "trip" or CB broke into the conversation just about the time Coot was getting to the good parts.

Then there was that first meeting with those big brown eyes, red lips and soft voice recalled from his first meeting with the new school teacher, Miss Morgan. Must have been a stagnant air inversion about that time as it was after midnight before it cooled down enough for Laroy to get some sleep.

"Laroy," a soft voice fought to break into his end of summer funk, "Laroy would you like to help me with my books? I have a lot of supplies for the new school year and they're are get'in awful heavy."

Feel'in like he was fighting his way out of a fog bank, Laroy turned to meet the gaze of none other than Ronda Sue. Flash back to summer at the swim'in hole and visions of "make believe" bringing back the memory of Coot having the image of CB and her bright yeller swim'in suit burnt on his eye balls all those years back.

Well, it may have been only "make believe" but right at the moment Laroy was having a terrible time clearing that bright lime green image from his eyes. "Laroy, are you OK?" the soft voice continued.

Standing stiffly to his full height, he replied, "why of course I am Ronda Sue, I think it's just another one of those stagnant air inversions, here, let me help you with those books."

Doesn't look like there are any trips to Pardon Us Mama lake for Fall fish'in, getting scheduled any time soon, but it seems like the once dynamic duo have both tak'in the bait. Can one or both manage to throw the hook? Stay tuned and see.

The Misguided Misadventures of Chinook and Laroy

Chapter 14

All in all, Laroy, still suffering and grieving about the previous summer's seemingly lost days, had persevered through the many hikes up the hill to Three Pines school, all the while laboring under the endless loads of books and school supplies that Ronda Sue somehow managed to burden him with.

Funny how she always seemed to appear just as the climb to Three Pines school transitioned into that last steep pitch.

He'd about given up walking with Chinook, his long-time friend, now seemingly otherwise occupied with daily loads of supplies ordered by Miss Morgan and dropped shipped from Mort and Sally's One of Everything Emporium.

With Miss Morgan's seemingly endless orders it was a wonder Chinook found room or strength to also carry Sally Mae's books and finished lessons all while not even accounting for his own books and lessons which of late had taken on a life of their own, growing in quantity if not quality almost daily.

Hadn't been one pig tail dipped in an ink well all year. Not one! In fact, if it weren't for the delicious and varied desert treats Ronda Sue had started bringing him every Friday, Laroy might have taken up with Jason Weiser, the son of the new Three Pines police Chief.

Jason, several years younger than Laroy, had moved to Three Pines with his father, Cal Weiser, mother Martha May, and four younger sisters, Marty, Mandy, Murial and the youngest, Martha May Jr.

Cal Weiser, Jason's father, had moved to Three Pines to take up the recently vacated post of police chief after a somewhat storied career as a State Fish and Game enforcement officer followed by a stint as a county sheriff's deputy. The terms of his dismissal as deputy still disputed, possibly having to do with the county's new hand held radar gun being damaged under rather questionable circumstances. Which Cal claimed involved a speeding mule traveling uphill at for all intents and purposes, an impossible rate of speed.

Anyway, it is probably just as well that Laroy was otherwise occupied and hadn't joined in with Jason's questionable antics. Antics which were beginning to make the folk of Three Pines long for the earlier and quieter days of Chinook and Laroy.

After the end of the calendar year school board meeting, rumors began to circulate that come Spring and the end of the current school year, at least one still un-named student and possibly two, would be advanced to grades more in line with their ages.

There had been some personal items switched around on back yard clothes lines, one garment even making it to the city hall flag pole, but failing to "fly" even in a good stiff breeze apparently due to its frilly construction. Best guess as to the failure was, it was hard for the wind to get a bite on something that lacy. Then there was the outhouse behind Missy's Grill & Suds that gave indications there had been an un-successful attempt to move the rather heavy 2 ½ hole unit.

As yet un-accustomed to the turning of a "new leaf" attributed in some quarters to Chinook and Laroy, others claimed that the once dynamic duo was up to old tricks. However, it was soon found and reported that during the times in question, Chinook was safely incarcerated in the living quarters of Mort & Sally's One of Everything Emporium and Laroy had left Ol'Coot's and CB's early in the evening on his way over to Ronda Sue's to do homework.

Has someone stepped in to fill the once active shoes of Chinook and Laroy? Time may tell, but mean while it seems for Chinook and Laroy, the "dynamics" may well have changed.

The Misguided Misadventures of Chinook and Laroy

Chapter 15

The foursome consisting of Chinook, Sally Mae, Ronda Sue and Laroy stood there in awe as Jason Weiser's old flat head V8, roaring and smoking finally broke the grip of the "slicks" loose from the pavement just moments before a resounding boom provided a clear indication that Jason would soon be making another visit to the back lot of Smith's War Surplus Things and Such or Short's Gas & Garage, Inc.

Clearly considering the Weiser boy's seemingly unquenchable thirst for the "slicks" found at those locations it was a good thing the dynamic Duo had never been drawn to the "motor sports."

Ronda Sue, looking up at Laroy with those captivating brown eyes said, "why I never! You and Chinook never did such disgusting and destructive things, now did ya?"

"What about you Sally Mae, you ever see a more childish display, and all just to draw attention to himself?"

"Not me," Sally Mae replied as she linked her arm to Chinook's.

"I'm so proud of Chinook and Laroy, I don't know about you, but I could never be seen with someone exhibiting such juvenile behavior as that!"

Glancing towards his long-time friend just in time to see Chinook give an embarrassed gulp as the color of his cheeks approached the level of a bad sun burn. Laroy stretched, began to adjust his suddenly overly tight collar figuring the less said the better at that point.

"Did you pick up that new 8 track tape?" Ronda Sue asks her friend.

"Yep," Sally Mae replied. "It came in with yesterday's shipment and mom set it aside for me."

"Well then," Ronda Sue replied as she attached herself to Laroy, guiding his clearly hesitant steps in the direction of the Three Pines community center. "I'm thinking another week or so of lessons and the boys will be ready for the prom dance. Few more evenings and my dress will be finished and the new petty coats arrived from Sears and Rarebacks last week. That dusty rose will look splendid with a white orchid shoulder piece."

Twisting his head from side to side as he stretched his neck, Laroy thought about just how uncomfortable his collar had become in the last few minutes. Must be the warm spring weather, a rise in the humidity or maybe another of those stagnant air inversions possibly coupled with that side long glance directed his way by Ronda Sue.

Increasing levels of "Make Believe," dance lessons, orchids, prom dresses and to think there was probably a spring fly hatch up at Pardon Us Mama. Almost, well it almost seemed it might be worth serving as Chinook's sometimes less than enthusiastic pack mule on another back-country fishing trip. Plus, last time he'd checked, he and Chinook still had a credit balance at Mort and Sally's One of Everything Emporium and Smith's War Surplus Things and Such, and he knew for a fact that there were still cases of Slammie just sit'in there in the stock room at Mort & Sally's, the use by date rapidly approaching.

Seems like Chinook wasn't anywhere close to using some of their credit to stock up with a few cases of Slammie for a back country trip, in fact just a couple days ago he'd seen his pal elbows deep in potting soil as Sally Mae provided her decorative expertise to guide Chinook's efforts with spring plantings to bright'in up the Emporium's entrance.

Chinook and Sally Mae planting Snap Dragons, Ronda Sue hinting about white orchids, a dress with a half dozen of those puffy petty coats and maybe his wearing something other than high top work boots being easier on her feet during the dance lessons, all that and not one fish'in trip in almost a year.

Having not quite decided if "make believe" was really worth all the changes he and Chinook had found thrust upon them recently, Laroy was deep in thought, concentrating on his steps as he walked towards Coot and CB's place when the chirp of the sheriff's siren broke into his thoughts.

Sherriff McMasters had no sooner pulled over, none other than Jason Weiser, when Cal Weiser the new Three Pines police chief, arrived under full lights and siren.

With Jason out of his old car, a blue haze drifting lazily skyward from the tail pipe, sheriff McMasters and the police chief quickly entered into an enthusiastic discussion.

I wonder, Leroy pondered as he continued towards Coot an CB's place still a couple blocks away, maybe I'll talk to Chinook about the possibility of getting our store credits transferred to Jason Weiser.

I don't know if he likes Slammie, but he does seem to be a likely candidate in need of some diversionary out of town activities.

"Hey Laroy," Coot hollered as his young friend opened the gate that CB insisted was a part of every respectable front yard, "Come sit a spell, I think I've got some helpful insights on "make believe." Might be useful for you and Chinook considering I'm hear'in rumors of a prom coming up."

Ol'Coot's Quiche

Please note, the better the sausage, the better the end result

I have used, little pig Sausages, as well as bulk sausage, but when I began to use the Falls Brand of smoked link sausage, the end result was much better.

I buy the Falls Brand link sausages at our local Wenco, but I suspect any good smoked link sausage would be good. Falls Brand sausage is made in Southern Idaho.

The Falls Brand sausage comes in a 24oz package containing 8 links, each about 1" in Dia.

Falls Brand sausage also has a hot version of their link sausage and this has also gone over very well.

6 cups frozen hash browns – shredded

15 eggs

2 cups cottage cheese

24 little pig link sausage cut into ½" pieces (see comments above)

1 can black olives (sliced)

1 lb. Grated cheddar cheese – SHARP

1 ¼ tsp. Baking Powder

2 tsp. +/- Tabasco Sauce

1 tsp. +/- chopped parsley

10X14" baking dish

Beat eggs with a whisk

Add baking powder, combining with eggs

Mix all ingredients

Pour into greased baking dish

Bake at 350 degrees for 50 – 60 minutes or until center tests done

ENJOY!!!!!!!!!!!!!!!!!!!

--- True Character ---

I've about had it, all this bad press about my beloved state of Ideeho is about to do me in. And to think that much of this is spread about by some back country North Ideeho "humorist," and I do use that term "humorist" loosely, with a strange sounding foreign name.

It's not that I have anything against people with strange foreign names you understand, but with that guys roots still planted on another shore, he tends to badly misrepresent this glorious piece of real estate that I call home.

His most galling misrepresentations have been about of his list of, "characters," both good and bad, and his tendency for exaggeration which he has paraded before an unsuspecting public for low these many years.

I just want to set the record straight once and for all, so that anyone reading his material, from here on out, will know it for what it really is, the literary wanderings of a North Ideeho wanna-be.

As I've already indicated, the list of people he has represented as "characters" have little of it. Character that is.

Except for that fellow Stretch, or whatever his name might be who I happened to meet in a local store one day, the rest of the group wouldn't even get a second-row seat around the barrel stove at Cully's – Logging and Sheep Herder Supply, Inc.

Let me tell you about a couple of those front row boys at Cully's. Most of them are verifiable third and fourth generation characters with some getting the trait from both sides of the family. In which case, they usually exhibit what is known in these parts as, "True Character."

In fact, around here, those that aren't at least second-generation characters are usually known as having "doubtful character," which is a subject we best not get into at this time and place.

Just to prove my point, I'll give you just a bit of back ground on Ol'Asgood Johnson a real true character if there ever was one. So highly was Asgood esteemed locally, he had held the title to first chair, front row over at Cully's for five years running and would most likely have remained in that position indefinitely if not for a bit of misfortune on his part.

Seems as though Asgood came down with a bit of a cold, nothing much really, or at least it wouldn't have been if he'd just taken time to read the label. As it turned out, Asgood ended up confined to the house for nearly a week, fearing that if he ventured past the front door, the lingering effects of the laxative he'd consumed, two tablespoons at a time, every four hours for almost two days just might disgrace the whole family.

Well, Asgood was so exhausted from all the exercise that before he could get back on his feet and regain the strength allowing him to return to Cully's, he'd lost his coveted first chair and nearly slipped into the second row.

However, knowing Asgood's reputation as I do, I'd guess he can be expected to regain the first chair position real soon because as far as character goes, he has it all over his cousin, Hound Dog Johnson who'd slipped into first chair during Asgood's absences. It's only a matter of time and the right diplomacy. Hound dog being from the side of the family where diplomacy really counts for something, not that their all that diplomatic themselves you see, it's just that they tend to monopolize family get togethers with their grievance procedure if things aren't handled just so.

Well anyway, as I indicated earlier, Asgood comes from that part of the family that is chock full of character. On both sides! For instance, there is Cindy Lou's daddy Ol'K.C. Banner that was head of the mule racing association down in Southern Idaho before he got himself some racing stock and had to resign his chairmanship due to a conflict of interest.

It was about the time that Cindy Lou left home to marry Asgood's poppa, that K.C. started to come up with what could have been some real winners. One in particular, a real stand out, was a young mare name of Molly Sue.

So far Molly Sue had left everything in the 2 and 3-year-old classes back at least 4 lengths in every race she entered, and never once did she even break a sweat. Be'in the optimistic type, K.C. figured she was just play'in with the local competition, so he decided to hire a trainer, pack up and head off to enter Molly Sue in the big money events.

Other then what had happened when Cindy Lou left home by way of an upstairs window, more about that later if time allows, things had been going pretty smooth for K.C. up to this point. But when he was only able to find one other mule racing association and that one clear back in South Western Missouri things started to go downhill.

Once they arrived in Missouri, the locals only let K.C. race Molly Sue one time at Missouri Downs. It might have had something to do with Molly Sue beating the local favorite so badly he refused to race again, but right after that race they hurried K.C.'s outfit out of town indicating they probably weren't interested in an Ideeho rematch.

Not one to give up, K.C. got to think'in that Molly Sue just might have a future pacing thoroughbreds back in the green hills of Tennessee, so after he wired the trainer money to bail Molly Sue out of the glue factory, the trainer had pawned her to meet expenses, they hit the road again.

Everything worked our fine for about two weeks, in fact it was just a week before the final big money race of the year, you know the kind where they have all the fancy parties, the big cars and fast women with the big hats, or is that fast cars and big women with equally big hats?

Anyway, when the two leading contenders for the biggest purses of the year had to take early retirement after trying to catch Molly Sue down the back stretch, it was decided that pace mules were a thing of the past in thoroughbred racing.

The only thing that really bothered K.C., about what seemed to be the end of Molly Sue's racing career, was the fact that he still didn't know just how fast she could run. So, having decided to keep the trainer on for a spell, he put his mind into some concentrated effort, hoping to find a solution to the problem.

Once they got back to Ideeho, the process just never seemed to jell and after just 3 sleepless nights, Ol' K.C. had just about decided to retire from mule racing, figuring to put Molly Sue out to pasture as the undefeated champion. That line of thinking had a good bit of merit and everything would have probably worked out OK if K.C.'s new neighbors hadn't picked that 3rd night to hold the house warming party to end all house warming parties.

K.C.'s natural let-em-be attitude had already put up with weeks of construction vehicles keep'in the dust stirred up on the county road. He hadn't even minded the steady process of catering vans for the last 2 days and in fact he'd kind of enjoyed the sight of those two big fancy tour buses mov'in by slow like last evening.

You know the kind, they've got those big murals painted along the sides and across the back, show'in All those places you can't afford to visit. He hadn't even minded too much when the country western band fired up about sunset on the outdoor stage they'd put up on the hill behind his barn. But along about 1:00am when that voluptuous female singer cat squalled her way into the 4th verse of a love gone wrong somewhere around Amarillo, K.C.'s attitude went critical.

At that point, it took Brenda Jo about 2 seconds to roll out of and under the bed. She'd seen K.C.'s attitude go critical only one other time, back when Benny Johnson, later to be Asgood's father got the wrong window two nights running while trying to elope with Cindy Lou. Anyway, once had been enough for Brenda Jo and she wasn't about to get in the way a second time.

It took K.C. just about that long to get to his old side by side shotgun stand'in in the corner. He picked up Ol'Maudie Ann, named after his grandmother, the first verifiable character on the Banner side, dropped a couple of loads of double o buck down the spout and headed for the door complaining about female singers and country music in general and mumbl'in something about it be'in about time for that gal to be part'in.

Anyway, it was about then that Brenda Jo took the opportunity to shriek, an action which caught K.C. completely by surprise.

He never was sure why it happened unless it had something to do with his favorite cat hound's nose and the dog having laid prior claim to the space under the bed. But that shriek, not normally be'in associated with the vocabulary of those possessing true character must have startled K.C. something fierce just about the time he got to the door.

K.C. went through the door about a half step out of sync, putt'in him into perfect position to slip the screen door hook into the button hole on the back flap of his summer weight long johns.

The time it took for the hook to tear its way out of the button hole in those long johns would have been just long enough to allow K.C.'s character to slip back out of critical, except for what happened next. When the hook finally let go, K.C. was, by that time, at least a full step out of sync and headed full tilt for a four-foot drop, off the edge of the back porch.

Trying to work in a little English back to the right, K.C. stepped smack dab in the middle of a pile of old mule shoes left over from Molly Sue's racing days. As luck would have it, the top shoe was laying there, nail side up which is exactly where K.C.'s left foot came down.

With 3 of those old nails embedded firmly in his left heel, K.C.'s understandably violent reaction caused him to clear the porch by at least 10 feet in his first jump. Then with the shoe still firmly attached and K.C. showing a bit of tendency to favor that foot, you can understand how he might have a bit of problem negotiating back yard obstacles in the pre-dawn darkness.

Ol' K.C.'s momentum had been picking up ever since the point of Benda Jo's shriek, so when he ran the toes of his right foot into the reel of the push mower it gave him just the boost needed to clear the back fence, tak'in his shotgun, Maudie Ann, mower, mule shoes and all with him.

Well, when he came down on the end of the old wood watering trough, he landed so hard he finally lost his grip on Maudie Ann putting her into a high arc lined up perfect like for Brenda Jo's back yard clothes line.

One thing having led to another, Maudie Ann hit the clothes line wire in such a way as to bring both hammers to full cock on the old side by side, just before she hit the ground. When Maudie Ann touched down, both barrels let go at once heading those charges of double o buck up and over the barn and out to where Molly Sue was just starting to dream about mov'in up to the starting gate for the biggest race of her career. Having been handed the baton, so to speak, Molly Sue was off and over the fence the moment those double o's touched down, and still gaining speed when she hit the highway just about 30 seconds later.

Well, it so happened that Cal Weaser, the local deputy, had picked just that time to be at the top of Sunset Hill testing one of those new-fangled electronic radar guns for the county sheriff. He had just got the thing set up and was start'in to figure out all the buttons, when he saw some lights coming out of dead man's corner at the bottom of the hill.

Not having a lot of faith in the new technology, Cal took aim at the approaching lights and pressed the trigger just as the vehicle was about to top the grade. Just as he got a reading, he looked over the top of the gun to check his aim only to find himself lined up on, you guessed it, Molly Sue. Now Cal know'in nobody was going to believe any mule do'in 95 in an uphill pass'in lane, threw the gadget down in disgust and headed back to town to begin what he figured to be about two weeks of administrative leave for destruction of county property.

Figuring it best to be leav'in out the finer points of what he'd just observed, Cal closed his daily report by saying that the subject was last seen heading South towards Elko at a high rate of speed, make and model unknown.

The Country Boy

There he sat, the country boy
A hick by any name
Hiding in a far back pew
Folk hardly knew his name

While cross the room a city girl
A few rows forward sat
She's casting glances towards the back
To where the duffer sat

He's sure not much to look at
This fellow from the hills
And surely not enough at best
To cause the girl some chills

But who's to know the outcome
These workings of the heart
Yes, stranger things do happen
Their wanting not to part!

City Girls and Country Boys

There they stood those city girls
Both dressed in fine array
While cross the room the duffer stood
Not knowing what to say

Those girls as fresh as daisy's
On such a fine Spring Day
Just in from miles distant
But not with long to stay

We'd seldom see the likes of those
In our small country town
For gals from farms in hills about
Come dressed for get'n down

They might have saddled horses
Or mucked out smelly stalls
Then jump'n in their peekup truck
Their out to make some calls

Yes, city girls or country girls
Are both a sight to see
While country boys are best with toys
With motors, could it be

So city bred or country fed
The mystery still remains
Those sweet young things surprises bring
While duffers make no gains

For duffer boys know not the ploys
Young ladies bring to bare
A smile warm, those lips so soft
Can't help but stop and stare

But once that door is opened
Resistance is in vain
For city girls or country girls
The outcomes still the same

Star and the Greenhorn

Remember back to days of yore, the Ol' truck headed East
A new beginning was ahead, to young eyes such a feast

From hills of green and trees in rows, to pine trees stand'in tall
Ahead lay miles, hill all brown and little else at all

The bunch grass short between the rocks, with sage all strewn
about
In twisted growth the pattern dark, those junipers did sprout

I'll need a horse to ride those hills, I'd read it in the books
Of days gone by and cowboys tall, hats low or'e desperate looks

You'll have a horse, my father's word, on that I could rely
So once arrived a search began, a horse we'd surely buy

A saddle, used, was found one day, in Prineville where they
shopped
To buy the oats a cow to feed, a pig we'd also slop

A trip we made to call again, the feed store where they'd been
That saddle yet to find a home, a rough out it had been

A padded seat in yellow bright, had brought it back to sell
Those laughing calls, a cowboy tall, the mix just didn't jell

A double rig that rough out was, the leather thick and strong
We headed home in our Ol' truck, the trip that day was long

Now down the road bout seven miles, on highway 26
There lived a family, ranchers they, the need of horse could fix

They had a gilding, bay it was, he stood bout fifteen hands
"Could sell you Star, he needs a home, there by the fence he
stands"

Soon there I sat, as green as grass, this youngster from the
west
That rough out firm upon the back, Ol'Star was sure the best

We headed out upon the road, those seven miles to go
The gilding tall, a-mov'in, calm, weren't mak'in any show

But up the road, around a curve, the road did strieght'in out
And Star by now all loosened up, decides to spread em out

That's when the mak'in of this tale, began to take a turn
With Star a break'in to a run, for something firm I yearn

I snug my legs up close to Star, he hunches up a bit
The grip on leather tighten's up, my hope is still to sit

Upon the back like cowboy tall, this bronc I've found to ride
Yet funny how my plans have changed, I'm fear'in for my hide

We're mak'in time, Ol'Star an I, he's mov'in swift and sure
While on his back I bounce and jolt, on rough out not secure

So, there it ends as on the ground, I suddenly did lite
My days of rid'in tall, were just of fancys flight

Yep, me and Star was part'in as to the barn we turned
Us both was now a-walk'in, one lesson I had learned

Before ya try a-sit'in, jus like a cowboy tall
It's best to be a-learn'in, while still your short and small

Or soon you'll be a-sitt'in, just like that greenhorn kid
Upon the ground a-hurt'in, and moan'in like he did.

In Search of Alpha Elk
- OR –
Some Got It and Some Ain't

Imagine if you will, the chorus line to end all chorus lines. A line of lovely ladies stretching out to three, four, yes even to five hundred yards in length. The gals individually moving with what must be an inbred grace and yet, in perfect harmony, each with the others.

Each member stylishly decked out in the briefest of skin tight outfits. Alike, yet at the same time, a size and shape to fit every imaginable taste and style. A review exhibiting what dreams are made of.

All participants shown, both singly and collectively at their very best, all the while the sensuous rhythm of their performance threatens to drive the on lookers far beyond their normal levels of insanity.

And somewhere in that long line of swaying bodies moved a great grandmother or maybe the great great granddaughter of a great grandmother. In charge of all planning and choreography for the entire review, in short, the #1 "boss lady" of all elk. "ALPHA ELK."

The quest to rid the herd of this saving influence had begun years before. Around a camp fire, not unlike other camp fires, when "the Chief," a title now passed to his grandson, tried to explain his theories on simplifying the annual effort to restock the freezer. As Chief saw it, doing away with Alpha, would make the sometimes-grueling task known as "elk hunting," as easy as taking candy from a baby.

Now, to keep things in context and prevent any long retired "officials" from getting any wild ideas about bending the statute of limitations, we'll just refer to that long-ago leader as "Old Joe." You may have known Old Joe, but probably by a long list of other names. Most of which his dear departed mother wouldn't have recognized.

Anyway, through some tricks of genetics, or possibly because of the long-term effects of Old Joe's camp cooking, the Chief's boys just never seemed to have what it took to pick up the reins and follow in their father's footsteps. This was indeed a sad fact, and one which became increasingly evident as Old Joe began to think about stepping down.

As Joe aged, the title just naturally lay semi dormant until, just in time, one of the boys married and brought a new genetic strain into the family. This union was followed in due time by the birth of a baby boy, who showed himself to be so bright, that even before his 15 th birthday almost everyone in the country had taken to calling him, Sonny." That there was an upturn in genetic quality was even apparent before the young feller had hit two years of age and Old Joe had immediately decided to christen the youngster, "Little Chief."

Now there was one "regular," which was always included in the aforementioned camp cooking of Old Joe, the concept of which could have passed on a fair amount of pocket change to future generations. Providing that is, had the family as a whole, been a bit more perceptive. In fact, it would more than likely have brought their entire life style to the level which most of us, would gladly become accustomed.

It is doubtful that this camp fire creation could be called a culinary masterpiece of any sort, but Old Joe, being a good bit more then persistent, did bring it to the level of a solid tradition. However, the only real food value anyone could find in his creation was in the gallons of maple syrup and fruit preserves required to put down a meal's worth of ----- "DOUGHGODS."

As mentioned, the food value of doughgods might have been in question, but never the exercise value. In fact, the long-lasting amount of exercise provided could easily be factored by the ratio of topping consumed. The ratio normally being about 2 to 2 ½ gallons per doughgod, depending of course on the physical condition of the campers and the freshness of the batch. If the doughgods happened to be on the stale side, say out of the pan for more than 5 or 6 minutes, what turned out to be, possibly their most useful function came into play.

Old Joe's creation happens to bare a remarkable resemblance to what later came to be a highly successful toy. The doughgods, being only about 3 – 4 lbs. heavier and a lot harder.

Joe always figured it was one of those slick haired fellows posing as the seemingly always present, "game Wardens" that stole the idea and sold it to the toy maker. He was especially suspicious of one of the local and not quite so slick enforcement officers, a fellow name of, "Cal Weiser."

Being knee deep in some sort of questionable enforcement activity, was considered by the locals to be a normal condition for Cal, and another story entirely. It is also something his ex-supervisors would just as soon I didn't bring up, at least until they've been able to enjoy a few more years of retirement.

Anyway, Joe's boys by an early age had developed a knack for giving one of those doughgods an underhanded flip that sent the disk off sailing through the woods, to ranges in excess of 200yds. or more, depending on wind direction and velocity.

Now when I mentioned that they would sail through the woods, that is exactly what I meant, Through the woods. Not around the woods, seldom over the woods, weight being a deterrent to elevation gain, but through the woods including through whatever happened to be in the flight path.

On one memorable outing, a stray dog made the mistake of dropping into camp about the time one of the doughgods turned stale. Now as I've already mentioned, there was not a lot of time which lapsed between fresh and stale. Stale being a condition which normally turned up with regularity during the course of most meals. This was especially true as Joe's wife became a bit older and slower on her feet. A situation which contributed to her decreasing ability to open and replenish with any speed the rapidly depleted fresh containers of syrup and jam. This doesn't even take into consideration clearing away the ever-mounting stack of empty containers.

Sensing that a "fresh" doughgod he'd just reached for was quickly declining in quality, one of the boys flipped the rapidly hardening disk into the air in the general direction of an open meadow. As luck would have it, this particular day, a stray dog chose to visit the camp and had, sometime in his past, come up with the idea that chasing disk like objects flipped in the direction of an open meadow was great fun. So, not knowing this disk to be a "hazardous waste" by product of Joe's camp cooking, the dog was instantly out from under the camp table in hot pursuit of the hovering object.

Making a grab for the now low flying doughgod, the dog promptly found himself rolling across the meadow, howling in great pain, only to end up upside down with 2 black eyes and stripped of every tooth in his head. Admittedly, the black eyes were a bit hard to see given the dog's coloring and especially since it was 5 days before the swelling went down enough for the poor thing to again see.

All during "Poor Thing's" convalescence, the name just kind of coming naturally, Joe's wife being of a kinder and much gentler nature, fed the beast by way of a straw. She would carefully and tenderly work the straw between the swollen and bleeding lips, dip the other end in a little puree of road kill then tilt it up and let the mixture run slowly, gently, into Poor Thing's mouth.

Even with his eyes closed, it only took Poor Thing about a day to pick up on slurping his meals through a straw, which in turn soon allowed him to rapidly regain the strength he lost from the traumatic incident. One thing leading to another, the weight gain ultimately leading to his name being shorted to just plain, "Thing."

Strange as it may seems, Thing seemed to know in some instinctive way that Old Joe was at the root of his present condition and he soon began to take every opportunity to remind Joe of the fact. Thing had also decided that there were a number of advantages, especially considering his complete lack of teeth, to the continued use of a straw for taking his nourishment. Therefore, it was soon considered normal to see Thing running around the home place with a straw or two tucked behind his ear.

Even old Joe finally figured he could live with the questionable habit, with a little help from the lady of the house of course. Live with it except, well. Except for the other use Thing found for his growing collection of used straws.

As I recall, it was about the middle of October. Old Joe had already been cleaning his shotgun and checking his stash of shot shells for the better part of three weeks, waiting impatiently for the annual noon opener of bird season. He must have brough that Ol' side by side to his shoulder a hundred times or more during those weeks, as he followed the flight path of an imaginary pheasant.

The big day finally arrived, the shell loops on the old faded game vest had been filled with their quota of shells and Joe was in the final countdown phase of the morning as he alternately polished his shotgun and paced the living room floor watching as the seconds tick down on the old mantel clock.

Just as the clock struck 12, Joe stepped through the door and into the back porch only to be greeted by the call of a wild quail followed almost immediately by the cackle of a departing ringneck pheasant. "Hotdog," he thought, "the season ain't 30 seconds old and I'm surrounded by birds before I even step off the porch."

Well, it was one of those days. Joe hot and exhausted, figured he must have walked 15 miles before he collapsed back on the porch just at dusk. 15 miles if he'd walked a mile and not one single bird to weigh down the game pouch in the back of his vest. As Joe sat there scratching his head and trying to figure out what went wrong with a seemingly perfect day, he began to replay the events of the afternoon back through his mind.

Birds, he'd heard plenty of birds. Birds on all sides of him. In fact, as he thought about it, he realized he'd seldom been out of hearing of at least some kind of game bird. He hadn't even seen any hunters during his long trek. Everything was perfect, not even one hunter who might have scared the game away. In fact, come to think of it, he hadn't seen a living thing all afternoon, except that is, for an occasional glimpse of Thing trotting along 3 – 4 hundred yards behind him. Was he losing his touch, what could have possibly gone wrong?

Suddenly, the loud clear call of a rising pheasant sounded just behind him, only this time it was accompanied by a warm gust of what smelled a great deal like road kill with strong overtones of dog breath. Turning towards the sound, Old Joe was just in time to catch Thing complete with an evil grin on his toothless lips, tuning up for another cackle on one of his straws.

Realizing he'd been "had" and his 15 miles had been for nothing, Joe immediately began to work on a name change for what had just become a real sore spot in his daily existence.

Lucky for Thing, Joe's wife came on the scene about that time, just in time in fact to find her husband chasing the dog towards the barn all the while hollering what to her ears sounded like "Blank Thing" alternating with, "Blank blank Thing."

Being as I've already indicated that Joe's wife was of a kinder and gentler nature, and also being very concerned about the quality and level of her impressionable grand children's education, she decided that renaming the dog again might not be a good move at that point. It probably being better to stay with just one name and thus avoiding the possible and reckless use of the less desirable adjectives to which Joe seemed prone.

However, setting the subject of Thing aside for the moment, it was indeed fortunate that Old Joe held on long enough to oversee the training of one of his grandsons, or this story might never have been told. Least ways, not without the possibility of stretching the truth a bit beyond the breaking point.

Meanwhile the progeny of Ol'Alpha is still out there, still making a fool of every person set upon the task of filling a freezer.

1 Tales of Cal Weiser Sheriff Very Ordinaire

Bzzzzzzzzzzzzz snap, Cal's new multi position preprogramed desk chair stopped reclining and locked into position #10, the locking required before the preprogrammed positioning of the embossed head rest could occur. Position #12 being almost fully reclined and used only for afternoon naps at which time the foot rest was enabled to move to and lock in one of its 3 positions, including feet slightly above head level.

The county commissioners, had at first baulked at the expense of the custom office chair, finally only relenting when Cal offered to pay for the custom embossed head rest out of funds taken from his termination settlement which came about after the somewhat questionable termination of his police chief position at Three Pines.

The delivery of the custom head rest had been delayed due to the requirements of having the custom embossing die handmade along with obtaining the cash bond required to assure the artist hired and charged with inlaying the 24-carat gold in the embossing didn't abscond with the gold foil before the job was completed.

"Officer Jason, where is my coffee? You know I require my coffee immediately upon arrival at the office. Officer Jason, did you hear me officer Jason?"

"Ya, right away paw. I'm almost finished with the comics from yesterday's paper.

Sure wish we didn't need to wait for the mail. That always make the comics come across as old news, the comic section be'in a day late and all. Means I can't read Sundays comics until I pick up the paper, Monday at the Post office. I'm thinking the mail lady just holds it back out of meanness. Likely wants to read the funnies before she puts the paper in our box."

"COFFEE!"

"Yes paw, right away paw."

"Last warning! That's Sheriff Weiser to you anytime we're out of the house.

Jason, do you hear me? One more time and you'll be demoted from special deputy assistant to the sheriff and back to custodian. You hear me? ---------- deputy!"

"Yes paw, coming paw."

It wasn't that the coffee wasn't ready, the new automatic 36 cup coffee pot, bought by Cal as an office warming gift to himself was programed to begin brewing the 6 cups of breakfast blend full bodied grounds at the stroke of midnight and hold it at just below boiling until 7am when 4.5cups of fresh "make up water" was automatically injected to the pot only moments before it throttled the temp back to a more drinkable level.

Simultancously reaching for his steaming coffee cup as he advanced the reclining office chair into position #11, one setting below full recline, Sheriff Weiser powered his chair to where he could extend his feet onto the padded desk top.

Sipping from the hot brew as the big toe on his left foot waved gaily to Miss Finchlaroy who just happened to glance through the large bay window of his new office, Cal looked pointedly towards the phone located on the back corner of his desk just as it completed its 9th ring.

"Deputy, you going to answer that or let it ring all day?"

"Good morning, Special Deputy Jason Weiser at your service what can I do fer ya?"

"Weiser!" Came forcefully through from the caller. "Put the sheriff on, now!"

"It's that councilman Foncenboogger paw. Ya want ta to take the call or should I take a message? Paw ya hear'in me?"

"Last time, you will address me as Sheriff Weiser, is that understood?"

"Yes paw, ya want to talk to Ol'boogger or not?"

"Sheriff Weiser here, how may I help you councilman Foncer?"

"Weiser, you have a problem!" In fact, you have a big problem and one which considering your past performance it would be best if you'd choose to resolve this situation before your afternoon nap. What's that noise, Weiser? Sounds like snoring. Weiser are you awake? Did you hear me Weiser?"

"No problem councilman. I have you on speaker phone and my special deputy is making note of your concerns. Is there anything else councilman Foncer?

"Yes, Weiser, matter of fact there is! What's that noise?"

"Noise, noise ----------- oh councilman you must be referring to the electric eraser special deputy Weiser has employed. Jason shut that infernal thing off. You were saying councilman Foncer?"

"Weiser, I just had a call from fish and game and their hopping mad. Another one of their moose decoys has disappeared and their game cam shows what appears to be the Burns boys having committed the theft. Third moose decoy this week and 4 elk decoys the week before plus the 6 White Tail buck decoys that disappeared 4 weeks ago. Weiser, you getting all this? It has to stop and stop now Weiser."

"Yep, special deputy has it all down. What was the name of the suspects again?"

"Burns, John and Peter Burns, you, --------------- Weiser are you on this?"

"Right away councilman, right away. Just have one little matter to clear up first.

Peter Burns, you know, older brother to that trouble maker John Burns dropped by late yesterday, about 2:35pm just before quit'in time and reported that someone had broken into their trophy room and absconded with their prime collection of full body White Tail mounts. Peter seems to think it was Muddy and Scouter Bovill, but someone had failed to change the batteries in their trail cam so it is only a guess. Peter said they'd pick up more batteries next time their out for a walk."

"Anyway, I've assigned special deputy Jason Weiser to the case and he's headed over to visit to Bovills' just as soon as he finishes up taking notes. Jason, did you shut off that eraser? Sorry councilman, I thought that snoring sound was still com'in from that electric eraser. My mistake. Jason!"

"Weiser ------------------ what's this ---------------- country treasure just dropped some invoices on my desk. One is from a garage out there in Dreary, billing labor for the installation of a lift kit and turbo charger on a county 4X4, second invoice is for installation of a high-performance exhaust system with racing bypass. And here's a third one just dropped on my desk for a set of high traction off road tires.

Weiser ------------- care to try and explain this?"

"Jason! Jason get in here!"

"Sheriff Weiser!!"

"Coming Paw, be right there as soon as I pick up my ride over at the paint shop.

Backwoods Audio dropped the rig at the paint shop when they were finished installing the audio system a couple days back. Smudgy put a rush on the paint job, said it would be ready this afternoon. Be right there Paw, shouldn't be more than an hour".

"By the way officer, Sheriff Weiser," Councilman Foncer continued, "I had three more citizens stop by to complain about the noise your hounds are mak'n. That is at least 5 complaints in the last two weeks and two citizens even filed official complaints, in triplicate, which means I must turn in the complainants to the commissioners. I can't side step the complaints when they are made in triplicate, which means your hide is likely to be nailed to the wall considering your employment probation has already been extended three times."

Sheriff Weiser makes a grab, for the phone beating deputy Jason to the desk phone by only seconds.

Sheriff Weiser speaking. You have problems, I have solutions. This conversation is being electronically recorded. Please state your name and location clearly for the record. How may I help you?"

"Sheriff Weiser, this is Olivia at the county switchboard. Sorry I was unable to get to your line earlier, how may I direct your call please?"

"Olivia, this is sheriff Weiser would you please patch me into the human resources office. I think we will be having an opening in the department. Could be soon."

#2 Tales of Cal Weiser

Two hours later, Deputy Jason Weiser returns to the Woodsville sheriff's office.

"Paw, take a look at the paint job. Paw--------------"

"Sheriff!" That's Sheriff Weiser to you, and by the way, care to explain why you left the office right when I was trying to answer councilman Foncer's questions about the modifications you had made to the counties peeekup?

"Paw hurry there's a flock of birds headed this way, they're about to land, get here quick before they do their thing on the new paint. PAW!"

"Sheriff Weiser!!"

"Ya paw, I get it, come quick. I'll try to hold the birds off!"

"Officer Jason, if I've told ya once, I've told ya 537 times! Unless ya want to be back in one of those stripped jumpers and push'in a mop, it is Sheriff Weiser to you!"

"I get it, I get it, you go'in to come look at my new paint job or not? Not sure how much longer I can keep the birds from landing on my custom light bar. PAW-------------."

"--------------------------------------- Officer Jason, just what is the point of having a high gloss metal flake paint job in a camo paint pattern? Doesn't the gloss and metal flake kind of defeat the idea of Camo? And, just how do you expect to pay for this? The county is already baulk'in at the turbo, lift kit and fancy tires on custom rims you had installed. I doubt they'll be impressed with your change from basic black to high gloss metal flake camo. How do you expect to pay for this and what about that custom light bar, did ma increase your allowance?"

"Naaa paw, ain't cost'in the county one red cent. Smudgy's trading the paint and light bar for a full body bull moose mount. Burns boys said they should be gett'in another shipment any day now and they'll drop ship it directly to Smudgy's house.

"What do ya think of my custom antennas? Guys over at Back Woods Audio had them special designed to fit the trucks décor. Did ya check out that cool interior?"

"PAW-------------------------------------- can ya park your peetrol car on the street until John and Peter Burn's get the addition built?"

"Besides that, me an the Burns boys got a little deal going. I don't ask and they don't tell. Maybe I should introduce them to the county commissioners. Might save the county a lot of money."

"Nooooooo! oh please tell me this is not happening, you are aware are you not Officer Jason, that you simply can't be making changes or additions to a county building without the commissioner's OK. You are aware of this fact, or aren't you?"

Ooooooooooooo! Yip Grrrrrrr yip Oooooooooooooooo -------------- ----------. "Officer Jason, OFFICER JASON get those hounds under control."

"Aaaaaaaah paw, I think We have a problem."

"Officer, what do you mean, 'WE' have a problem? Can you control those hounds or not?"

"Aaaaa well, you see when I ask you to move your pretrol car to the street last night so my peeeekup with the new paint could be under cover overnight, well last night I needed a place for Ralph and Sooner to bed down so I put them in the garage with your car and kind of opened the doors so they could get inside and be comfortable and warm and ------------- well, it must have been something they ate."

"Sure glad Smudgy suggested leaving my peekup in his shop one more night"

"Officer, what do you mean it must have been something they ate?"

"Well Paw------------."

"Sheriff!"

"Yes Sir, Sheriff Sir, I'd suggest you call the county shop and have someone bring out the counties pressure washer. Your car and -------------- and part of the garage might need to be cleaned a bit and ------------------."

"So now I need to have someone come out and clean up a mess, which reminds me officer, I had three more citizens stop by to complain about the noise your hounds are mak'in. That is at least 5 complaints this week and doesn't count last week's complaints. Two more official complaints, again in triplicate, and I'll remind you again, being as how they filled out official complaints, I'll have to file them with the commissioners. I Think you'd be wise to look for other employment."

"Ah Paw, ------------------"

"I'm a think'in there is a high likelihood you are better suited to go back to delivering pizza for the Woodsville bar and grill and just where are the Burns boys coming up with a full body moose mount this time of the year? Answer me that will ya!"

"Ah Paw, you know I -------"

"That is Sheriff Weiser to you officer and if you won't tell me, I'll have your ma wring it out of ya. One way or the other officer Jason, I going to find out."

"The local fish'n and game officer dropped in couple days back ask'in if I knew where the Burns brothers were hang'in out. Seems some lady filed a complaint about her pet moose come'in up missing about the same time John Burns was seen in the area."

"I'm a-tell'in ya officer Jason the county fathers get one more complaint that leads back ta you and no matter how persuasive your ma is, you'll be back to deliver'in pizza."

"Ah Paw ----------------"

"That is Sheriff Weiser to you officer, now get the mop and finish the floor ya started last week, I don't care what your ma said. She ain't your boss no matter what she might think! Get that floor finished or your truck will be parked on the street."

"Ma ain't go'in ta like this and I'm tell'in soon as I finish the floor."

#3 Tales of Cal Weiser

"Calvin Sabastian Hugo Weiser IIII, what's this I hear I about you tell'in Jason Alvin Weiser to mop the floor down at the Sheriffs office? You know little Jason can't stressing his back do'in such meaningless work. You know his delicate condition after he scored the winning touchdown at the state Jr. High football tournament."

"Now Martha May --------"

"Don't you be Martha May'in me Calvin Sabastian you just lay off'in little Jason, how dare you assign'in your son to such menial tasks as mop'in floors in your office. How dare you know'in Jason's weakened condition."

"Marthie, that game was almost ten years ago an the doctor said -----------------"

"Calvin Sabastian you know I hate when you use "Marthie", especially in that tone of voice. My name is Martha May Hillebrand Weiser. Besides what does that doctor know? You men all stick together and even with all that book learn'in don't mean that doctor knows everything."

"You send Jason Alvin home right this minutes, it's time for his nape."

"Yes ---------------------"

"Don't you be yes'in me, just send my son home right this minute. You hear me?"

"I'll have some warm milk waiting to help him get to sleep!"

"Who was on the phone paw?"

"Who was on the phone ---," Sheriff Weiser.

"Ya paw, who was it?"

"You got that floor mopped yet Deputy?"

"Ah paw ---."

"Don't "ah Paw" me. That was your ma and she thinks you need to come home for a nap, although for the life of me and with no more than you've accomplished today I can't see why you need a nap. You didn't report for duty until nearly 10:30. By the way just where were you?"

"I suppose you were meeting with John and Peter again. Those Burns boys are really giving the city of Woodsville a bad name. I thought Chinook and Laroy were bad when I was a police officer over at Three Pines, but they don't hold a candle to these Woodsville boys. I'm tell'in you deputy Weiser those boys are trouble and they're going to suck you into the hole with them. Maybe you should think about it while you're taking your nap."

Just about the time Sherrif Weiser leaned back in his custom recliner, the office door burst open slamming the door into the wall with enough force to crack the window in the door, third time that month.

"Sherrif Weiser, is that no good worthless son you call a deputy hiding out anywhere close by?"

"Why Mrs. McConnel, Just how can I help you on such a fine afternoon. Beautiful Spring Day don't ya think? Great day for a walk. How may I help you?"

"Now don't you be fine day'in me Weiser! Just tell me where I can find that lazy county employee, my tax money is helping to pay his wages and I going to talk to the county commissioners about the waste of tax payer money! I suppose he's hanging around with the rest of those worthless Woodsville boys. Talk about worthless, those no account Burn's boys take the cake in that department."

"Be that as it may, I'm here to file an official complaint with the county. Those boys, all three of them snuck down to the swimm'in hole last night, about midnight and made off with all the clothes of my daughter and her three friends."

"My daughter and her friends had to sneak home neked as the day they was born. My Sally Jane has skeeter bites over every square inch of her body, not even considering the embarrassment of being seen by Ol'Ruppert Hawkins in the alley behind Cindy's bar and grill."

"Word is already out all over town about the girls com'in home neked in the middle of the night and the phone ain't stopped ring'in all morning. Sally Jane has already had offers of five dates to go swimm'in tonight, but until the swelling goes down from the skeeter bites she ain't likely to be going anywhere. and Ol'Ruppert is getting free beers every time he retells his story down at Cindy's. What ya going to do about it?"

"Well, Mrs. McConnel, I don't rightly know there is much I can do. I suppose I could go on a stakeout and make sure no one steels the girl's clothes again."

"Course I'm not sure how happy the county will be paying for the overtime on a stakeout just to watch out for some clothes. As per the whereabouts of deputy Weiser, there was an urgent matter he had to address at home."

Three days later -------------- "Good morning, Sherrif Weiser speaking. How may I help you?"

"----------------- Weiser, this is Councilman Foncer. We need to talk, NOW! I'd suggest adjusting that fancy reclining chair of yours to position number one."

"Yes, Sir Councilman Foncer, Sir. I'm at your service, Sir. How may I help you?"

"Weiser I just read the complaint form summited by Mrs. Gracy McConnel three days ago, but not before I received an irate phone call at 7:30am, this morning, stating that you Sherrif Cal Weiser have been sneaking down to the local swimming hole along about midnight and spying on her daughter and friends while they're skinny dipp'in in the crik."

"Not only that, but she reported that last week sometime you confiscated all the girls cloths and they all had to walk home naked, as the day they was born."

"And if'n that was not bad enough, I have in my hand a request for overtime pay for a stakeout you decided to run down at the crik."

"Mrs. McConnel was a little bit excited, but somehow it seems that the worthless deputy of yours is also involved along with those no good Burns boys."

"And while I have you on the phone, the Captain over at the Fish and Game office called again about some illegal game pouching in your district. Seems every time they are ready to make a move and arrest the perps, somehow they get tipped off and are long gone. They thought they had the culprits cornered one night last week but everyone had cleared out just minutes before they arrived. One of the officers saw a tricked-out pickup leaving the area in a cloud of dust."

"However, his description of the vehicle seems to resemble some invoices submitted from your office. Pickup with a lift kit, oversized tires with chrome rims, enough antennas the rig looked like a porcupine, but the clincher is the rig had a high gloss camo paint job with, now get this, there were metal flakes in that camo paint job. Can you believe a camo paint job with metal flake? High gloss no less!"

"I'm beginning to think there is a lot of truth in those stories I've heard about your time over at Lone Pine. I used to think it was just stories until I talked to a sheriff friend of mine who told me that when you worked for him, you tried to claim you'd clocked a mule at over 90mph with one of their new radar guns. On top of that, you claimed the mule was running up hill in a passing lane. He said no one shed any tears when you left his office a few weeks later and took the job over at Three Pines."

"Weiser, one more thing, as of today your deputy is terminated. Collect all his gear and the keys to his truck by the end of today. But for the life of me, I don't know what the county sheriff's department is going to do with a pickup with a camo metal flake paint job."

4 Tales of Cal Weiser

"I'm home ma. Where's the warm milk you promised?"

"Jason Alvin you get in here right this minute, and I mean NOW!"

"Yes ma, com'in ma."

"Jason Alivn Weiser, what's the meaning of all these phone calls? It's a girl call'in never the less! Get your body in here. Just who is this Ethal Candy Oliver?"

"Don't know any Ethal Candy Oliver ma. What's she want'in?"

"Likely story you not know'in this gal. Says you have some clothes that belong to her and Sally Jane McConnel and some other girl they's been hang'in round with this Summer. Swim'in suit, un-mentionables, jeans, tenny runners. Top of that, she says you made off with her clothes along with the clothes belonging to the other two girls when they were swin'in about midnight a couple days back. Says they had to sneak home neked, not a stich on!"

"Weren't me ma."

"Well, if it weren't you, just who was it? Those worthless Burns boys I suppose. Word has it they're the ones sneak'in into the Campbells place and fish'in out their pond."

"Weren't John and Peter ma! I was with them an we's was cleaning up the full body moose mount they pulled out of the ditch earlier in the day. Didn't finish up until nearly 2 in the morning. Maybe pa, I mean Sherrif Weiser, knows something about Ethal Candy's clothes. I seen some frilly things dry'in in the back room of the office. Back where he keeps the evidents for ongoing investigations. Saw them when I was in the back room getting the mop before com'in home for my nap, by the way, where is that warm milk?"

"Your warm like is on the kitchen counter, likely cold by now, I'm call'in your pa."

"Better call him, Sheriff Weiser, ma. He's gets really owly if he ain't addressed proper."

"Just you never mind Jason Alvin."

"Sherrif's office, Sheriff Weiser speaking."

"Calvan Sabastion why are there ladies' frilly undergarments hang'in in the back room of the sheriff's office?"

"Ah Marthie, you know as the county sheriff there are ongoing investigations I can't discuss with just anyone, even family."

"I ain't Marthie and I'm getting phone calls about someone mak'in off with clothes down at the crik when some girls were at the swim'in hole middle of the night. Seems it was the same night you were supposedly on stake out. Ethel Candy Oliver's mother called, and seems Ethel and a couple other girls went skinny dip'in and someone swiped all their clothes."

"Can't go into that right now, sorry. Did Jason get home? His peekup ain't moved- ------- sheriff's office how may I help you? Hold please ----- Marthie I have Mrs. Oliver holding on line 2, I'll call you back."

"Yes, Mrs. Oliver, how may I help you?"

"Sheriff Weiser, I was just speaking with Councilman Foncer. I told him my grandson could do a better job as sheriff than you do. What are you going to do about the Burns boys, not even to mention that worthless deputy?"

"Councilman Foncer said the council will be addressing my concerns at the next business meeting and by the way the Burns boys just shot up another game department decoy. Are you there Weiser, are you lessoning? What is that beeping sound Weiser ------beep beep be-----?"

"Back at ya Marthy, what's up? Is Jason home yet?"

"Calvin Sabastian, I think you need to retire. I'm get'in really tired of be'in hauled off to half the little podunk towns in Ideeeho, just so you can add another police chief or sheriff's badge to your collection. And yes, Jason is home. I gave him a cup of warm milk and put him down for a nap."

"About my suggestion that you retire, I overheard a conversation at the lady's stich and chatter meeting Monday afternoon, and Commissioner Foncher's wife was saying that the county commissioners are talking about throwing a big party in your honor, bringing in people from Three Pines and the department close to where they did that mule racing. Commissioners figure having people share first hand stories about you, such things as you setting up a speed trap for a mule in an uphill passing zone would add color to the festivities."

"Mrs. Foncer was saying that it seems they are having a problem finding anyone willing to go on record about your past or even that they knew you. The city clerk of Three Pines hasn't answered the commissioner's calls or letters, but that party would be a good time for you to officially retire."

"You could invite people like the Woodsville mayor and the town council members and other people you've worked with over the years, maybe even the John and Peter Burns and the other Woodsville boys. Seems like your always involved with them for some reason or other, even providing overnight lodging for them on more than one occasion. You're always talking about their antics and the trouble they get into. Even invite the local game warden and maybe if he meets those characters, he might be able to solve the cases you haven't be able to solve. What about if I drop a hint at the next Stich and Chatter meeting that you thinking about retiring?"

"Now Marthy, let's not get ahead of ourselves, I need to be thinking about your suggestion. Not sure I'm ready to retire just yet. Someone needs to solve the disappearance of the game department decoys and the matter of those girls' cloths disappearing in the middle of the night and ----------."

ring – ring - ring ----- "Good afternoon, Sherrif Weiser at your service, you have a problem, I'll find a solution, how may I help you today?"

"Weiser, do you ever get out of your recliner and go on patrol? I can't remember calling you once when you weren't in the office. Be that as it may, I think I'm hearing some welcome rumors, which if true will save the county a lot of paper work. Are you retiring?"

"Ah well a – a – a – a – aaaaa commissioner Foncer, I'm not sure about this retirement thing. It may be more of an ugly rumor started by some of the women at the local Stich & Chatter gathering a week or so ago."

"Well Weiser, let me put it to you this way, not only would your retirement, ASAP, save the county a lot of paper work, but quite possibly some embarrassment on your part. Embarrassment over things like, how did the clothes belonging to those girls who decided to take a midnight swim, end up in your evidence room? Then just who authorized the camo paint job on the county pickup not to mention the light bars, custom stereo and speakers, the lift kit, big tires and chrome rims etc. etc.? In fact, I'd suggest you find a place at your house for that custom recliner and do so in the near future."

"In talking to the other commissioners, we all agree that your retirement will smooth the attempts to save everyone involved a lot of questions an embarrassment, should it happen in the near future. Make up a guest list and we'll get er done, how about three weeks from today the second Tuesday of next month? By the way, your deputy's notice of termination is in process."

Three weeks later, the a retirement celebration in honor of sheriff Calvin Sabastion Weiser, better known as Cal Weiser, began promptly at 7"oopm Pacific standard time, in the grade school cafeteria in the town of Woodsville, Idaho.

"Good evening everyone, the members of the county board of commissioners are very pleased to welcome you to this joyous celebration. We especially wish to welcome our speakers this evening, the first of which is, officer R. F. Lattchet, who is representing not only his department and the newly elected county sheriff of that Southern Idaho county, but also the remaining members of the once active Idaho Mule Racing Association. Following officer Lattchet we'll welcome Chinook and Laroy, members of the city council in the little village of Three Pines, Idaho. And for those of you who may not know, Three Pines in located in some of the most beautiful high mountain country of Idaho."

"We'll hear from each of these gentlemen shortly, but first the members of the board of commissioners and each of the department directors throughout this county wish to present this commemorative plaque to Cal Weiser, sheriff very ordinaire. Sheriff Weiser, would you please step forward to except your plaque along with your official retirement papers."

"Thank you, Calvin, I gives me great pleasure to present you with your official retirement papers, but now if you'll please return to your seat I'm honored to introduce all the way from Southern Idaho, officer R. F. Lattchet, better known to his department as "Latch." Latch, welcome to North Ideeeho."

"Thank you, commissioner Foncer, I bring greetings on this joyous occasion from my department. Joyous I might add as I take this opportunity to present this long overdue bill to Calvin Weiser for willful destruction of county property, namely one new hand-held radar gun. Admittedly the story may have become a bit clouded in the years since the occurrence, and yes, possibly a bit embellished."

"However, the story goes something like this, Southern Idaho had at one time, as commissioner Foncer already mentioned, an active mule racing association. So active in fact, that one of their mules was banned from racing in the national mule races due to the fact that there wasn't a mule anywhere in the country that could keep up with her. But on with the story, this occurrence took place shortly before the associations last days in Idaho."

"Seems officer Weiser was assigned to test out some technology totally new to the small department. Namely a handheld radar gun. Located on the highway a few miles out of town is a long grade with a passing lane on the uphill side. "Wizy" a he was commonly referred to among department personal, decided the long uphill grade would be a good place to test the new technology. According to the report I found in the files, it wasn't long after Wizy set up at the top of that grade, that according to his report, he saw a vehicle round the curve at the bottom, clearly exceeding as the story goes, the 55MPH speed limit. Now, from this point onward, I need to put bits and pieces of department lore, coming from various sources, together with Wizy's sketchy report to have some idea of just what happened that day."

"Apparently Wizy lined up on the speeding vehicle with the new radar gun, tracking it in the view finder until it almost reached the top of the grade, at which point he triggered the sensor, locking in the recorded speed. Thinking he had a solid reading on the speeder, Wizy lowered the new fangled contraption only to find himself eyeball to eyeball with one of those racing mules, doing according to the radar gun, 95mph in an uphill passing zone. Pretty much disgusted with this new gadget, Wizy threw it down and drove off leaving it where it fell, laying alongside the road. That pretty much concludes the tale, except for the final entry in Wizy's daily report, which stated that the speeding "vehicle" escaped un- apprehended, make and model unknown."

"Again, my department wishes to thank you for this opportunity to set the record straight and present the repair bill for the damaged radar gun to Cal Weiser."

"Thank, you Officer Lattchet, this has been most informative. Now I want you to welcome a couple of longtime friends, both of whom grew up in the small town of Three Pines, Idaho, both now serving on the town council. Known simply to everyone as Chinook and Laroy, we welcome you. Please come forward and share some more of our retiring sheriff's most interesting history with us."

"Thank you, council members, for your most gracious invitation to help celebrate the retirement of the one-time police chief of Three Pines, Cal Weiser. As already stated, Laroy and I have been pals for a long-time spending most of our growing up years in and around the small town of Three Pines, that is when we weren't off trekking to one of the high mountain lakes to fish and camp."

"Our recollections of the Weiser family run more to our contacts with Jason Weiser, who along with the family moved to Three Pines when Jason was in the 8th grade, Laroy and I being in our senior year of high school at the one room school house. Moving to Three Pines from a larger community, Jason had trouble fitting into the life style of our laid-back community. Where Laroy and I were just beginning to relate to girls, while still more at home in the surrounding mountains, Jason was into driving fast an noisy cars up and down main street in an attempt to impress the girls of the town."

"The girls Laroy and I eventually married were still busy attempting to teach the two of us how to tie our ties, put our shoes on the right feet, and not step on their feet at the school prom, all while Jason was making the worse antics the two of us could dream up, look like fun events at a Sunday School picnic. With that, I'll turn the mic over to Laroy, letting him tell you how Jason's actions ended Chief Weiser's career as police chief of Three Pines."

"Good evening and thanks for the invitation to these festivities. In the interest of not being overly unkind to the honoree, I'll relate tales, of which there are many, in which Jason was the main figure of interest. Rumors indicate that Jason may have gotten older, but other than that he hasn't changed a lot, still tending towards loud and fast vehicles. This occurrence took place when Chinook and I were in our last year of high school. In fact, we were still being groomed, or maybe I should say made fit, with the help of our future wives, to be seen in polite company. "

"We happened to be at the community center, taking dancing lessons from our girlfriends, on the evening of this occurrence, about 9PM as I recall, when the towns fire alarm sounded. Seems Jason had climbed the fence on his way into the back lot of Short's Gas and Garage, looking for more tires or car parts, and while in the process of making his way over the 8ft. fence, dropped the gas lantern he planned to use while searching for the needed parts. Other than breaking and entering into Short's property everything had apparently gone according to plan until that point. Unfortunately, the fuel cap on the lantern had apparently not been tightened properly, allowing it to pop off and spill the full tank of white gas into the dead grass behind Short's garage."

"Everything may have been OK, were it not for the fact that Jason struck a match while looking for the fuel cap, which ignited the gas fumes setting the tall dead grass instantly on fire. Had the fire been confined to Short's back lot which contained little more than old wrecked and junk cars, everything might have passed without much being said. However, Short's property was adjacent to a field of about 20 acres also full of tall dead grass which adjoined a hay field full of recently cut and drying hay which burnt along with a large barn used to store cut and baled hay."

"Things in Three Pines were a little exciting that night, Chinook and I even being allowed to postpone our dance lessons until the next evening. Other than dealing with the insurance company which insured the farmer's barn and brought the state fire inspector into town, the loss of some dead grass and some old tires in the back of Short's Gas and Garage was no big thing. Nothing was going to be missed other than the possibility of some those tires fitting Jason's hot rods and were maybe his reason for climbing into the back lot to begin with. It was generally thought that the fire really cleaned things up on that side of town."

"However, what gave the whole incident a new meaning was when the fire inspector happened to find a gas lantern laying on the ground of Short's back lot. It was badly burnt, so you might think no big thing, probably been laying there for years. Except on closer examination of the lantern there was found an engraved brass plate attached which said, " Awarded to Calvin Weiser" the plaque also listing a date just two years earlier. That pretty much concludes my comments other than to say that Police Chief Weiser resigned as the Three Pines police chief 2 days later."

"Thank you, gentlemen, for providing these candid insights into the past of our outgoing sheriff, Cal Weiser. I believe this concluded the official part of this retirement celebration, feel free to eat your fill of the food provided and chat with friends as long as you desire. I'll end my comments with this one announcement, if any of the Oliver or McConnel families are present this evening, there are a couple of boxes by the door into the cafeteria containing an assortment of young ladies' clothes, which somehow found their way into the sheriff's evidence room. Thanks for coming, enjoy the rest of your evening."

What Lights Your Way?
A Christmas Reading

We hear of Rudolf with his shinny nose
a guide for Santa's sleigh
A magical thing on a stormy night
was a light to show Santa's way.

Now Santa comes but once a year
then he fades from thought and view
That jolly Ol'Man, white beard and red cloths
just weeks does it take for his due

But what of the star which shinned that night
to light the wise man's way
A guiding light to show the path
to a Savior who was born that day.

Yet today there are lights and not hard to find
from the tiny to the big and the bright
They glow and they sparkle, they wink and they sway
all colors, fashioned just to give light.

So with lights all about in all shapes and all sizes
why is it we can't find our way
We falter, we stumble, we seek but can't find
Though we search, we still struggle and stray.

Could it be that our searching is mostly in vain?
are the lights just window dressing?
Have our eyes been so blinded by the glitz and the bling
gaining little, while we live without blessing

Have we missed our direction, have we lost the clear path
have our feet been guided by ease?
Has the darkness about us made our search oh so hopeless
days filled with torment, can no one we please?

If you find yourself hampered with nowhere to turn
well friend, you're not all alone
For the many and mighty are on the same path
while the star and its message, they claim not for their own.

In spite of our wealth of learning, we missed it
the star and the manager of old
Which lead those still wiser than we seem to be
to seek, and to bring gifts of fine gold.

For there was born on that day the light of the world
just a wee tiny baby you say
but the one who still lives, of whom we have read
the one who awaits us today.

A Savior, a guide, a light for long paths
a hand although ageless, still reaches
to make the way clear, give a hand when its needed
The One of whom scripture still teaches.

So yes, there is light, through ages not dimming
it is there to be found, still today
The Savior of old still waits for you friend
with a hand, and a light for the way.

About the Author

Yes, what about the author now living out the days of his 82nd year, and what about the books, now with the pages you hold in your hand, numbering three?

Well, the author's story began in Klamath Falls, Oregon during a much simpler and more self-sufficient time. An only child, born to hard working and loving parents, some of my earliest memories are of my mother reading from the pages of such things as Sugar Creek Gang adventures.

As I began to read for myself, I developed a love for the stories woven through the pages of many books. I recall as a young reader, rushing to make sure I was into a new chapter when mom called lights out, knowing that mom would allow me to finish that chapter.

About the time I finished the second grade, we moved to Salem, Oregon where I was plunged into life with many aunts, uncles and cousins. Even though mom's very large family was widely scattered, there were many members living in the surrounding area. Mom, being the next to the youngest of 23 siblings. Can you imagine a family reunion, held at a church camp ground, numbering 400 or more? Oh, such wonderful times!

Living in the Salem area until I was about 14, we moved to Eastern Oregon, with the hope that the dryer climate would relieve some of my father's pain brought on by a life time of hard work.

Living at Mountain Creek Café on highway 26. We were located 7 miles from the nearest neighbors, neighbors who happened to be cousins and family. The Frankie's living another 10 miles from Dayville, our nearest small town. This time being the inspiration for what, years later, became the piece of cowboy poetry, "Star and the Greenhorn".

My father died during my senior year of High School, after which mom and I moved to John Day, Oregon to be closer to work, and were I began my work history, first at a small grocery store and then with the US forest Service.

It was during this time I met the love of my young life, bringing about a move to Pullman, Washington and beginning a long and varied work history. Almost becoming, the "jack of all trades and master of none".

The "varied" work history included but was not limited to, grounds keeper in city parks, utility worker which included everything from snow plowing to painting the fleet of city vehicles, vending machine service at Washing State University, to Licensed hazards waste incinerator operator, to grounds shop mechanic, garbage man, to even a few years as owner/operator of a Portrait/Wedding studio. Yes, it is a bit of an understatement to say my work history was varied.

Books, how did that happen? As already stated, I've had a long love affair with the printed page, seldom without one or more books in process of being read, but I can't remember just what began the journey that became the first novel, "Parts of the Whole."

Many of the early pages were "roughed" out in an old green three ring binder in which I would, day after day during lunch breaks, write out the basic story line of what would, over some years become a completed novel.

Were the writings confined to only the early pages of the novel? No. Coming from a very musical family background, there were many gospel songs written, some of which went on to the point of being set to music.

Enter the computer age, maybe better said just barely entering the computer age, but not saying I became computer literate. Barely being able to make the technology work at best, but I bought an old used PC from WSU surplus for the purpose of using it for word processing.

Slowly that first novel began to take form, little by little being taken from the rough hand written pages of the three-ring binder and put into the hidden recesses of that big gray box.

"Parts of the Whole", is a story about life lived out by many people, loosely based on the scripture found in Romans, 12: 4 – 8, the reader is encouraged to reject the sinful life with its pain and torment, and embrace the love and forgiveness of a Holy and Loving God, becoming in this way part of the whole.

"Yea Though I Walk," a sequel to the first novel, is a continuation of the first book, set about 20 years later and referencing the 23 Psalm. The characters in this work continuing to live out life, sin and salvation, good and bad, with the ramifications each choice brings.

"Ideeho Tall Tales, Etc." began when I first became acquainted with two fellows, who had grown up together, eventually, becoming brothers in law, and some of the crazy adventures they'd shared. Chinook and Laroy, the nick names they had long used, became the main characters in the series about the greatly embellished tales of what might have been.

"Etc." is meant to include the other misc. writings included within these pages.

I hope the tall tales bring you some healthy laughs and as much enjoyment as I received from writing the tales.